of

KEY SKILLS IN INFORMATION TECHNOLOGY LEVELS 2 AND 3

P.M. Heathcote, B.Sc. (Hons), M.Sc.
R.P. Richards B.Sc. (Hons), M.A.

Published by

PAYNE-GALLWAY
PUBLISHERS LTD

26-28 Northgate Street, Ipswich IP1 3DB
Tel: 01473 251097 • Fax: 01473 232758

www.payne-gallway.co.uk

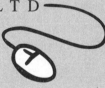

Acknowledgements

We are grateful to QCA for permission to reproduce the Key Skills Specification.

Cover picture © 'Mountain Clouds'
by Kirstie Cohen

Cover photography © Mike Kwasniak,
160 Sidegate Lane, Ipswich

Cover design by Direction123.com

First edition 2000.
Reprinted 2001, 2002, 2003.

Second edition 2004

A catalogue entry for this book is available
from the British Library.

ISBN 1 904467 51 2
Copyright © P.M. Heathcote and
R.P. Richards 2004

096485853

Printed in Great Britain by
W.M. Print, Walsall, West Midlands

Preface

Why gain an IT Key Skills qualification?

Information technology (IT) now pervades almost every aspect of modern life. Few people have no dealings with it and for many an ability to deal effectively with it is often the means to success. A willingness and ability to embrace information technology is becoming a prerequisite for successful modern life.

This second edition has been updated to reflect changes in the specifications and portfolio evidence required. MS Office 2003 has been used throughout, but users of earlier software versions will have no difficulty in following the instructions.

Purpose of this book

This is not a book for the IT specialist. It aims to present teachers and students of this subject with the basic technical information required in order to become proficient in the skills identified in the specifications for IT Key Skills levels 2 and 3. This includes work with software application packages such as word processing, spreadsheets, databases, presentation graphics and desktop publishing as well as use of the Internet and e-mail. It also includes the development of skills in finding and selecting information and project planning together with an appreciation of the implications of working with IT.

The requirements of the Key Skills specification are often expressed in a very generalised way. This book interprets these requirements in a practical, hands-on way and leaves teachers and students in no doubt as to what is required. For example within each chapter, advice is given on how the requirements of the specification are met by the activity in question, the evidence to be collected for a particular activity and sample questions etc.

Although primarily written as an aid for students and teachers of IT Key Skills, it will also be a useful text for students on many IT courses such as GCSE IT, to assist in their practical project work.

Extra web site resources

Please look at our web site www.payne-gallway.co.uk/ksit for valuable extra resources, such as answers to the questions at the end of each chapter, files to be used in some of the sample tasks in the book, portfolio recording sheets and sample portfolio work.

For additional teacher's resources follow the link from www.payne-gallway.co.uk. For example you can download the Overhead Transparency Masters which are provided to accompany each of the chapters in this book. They are for use by teachers to summarise the underpinning knowledge required.

Sample schemes of work are also available. These demonstrate one method of delivering the IT key skills syllabus over one academic year, starting from the assumption that the skills will be taught in 1 hour sessions over approximately 30 weeks. Although it is recommended that students begin to collect portfolio evidence as early on in their course as possible, the sample schemes of work allocate several weeks of contact time for the production of additional evidence towards the end of the course.

Table of Contents

Part 1

Information Technology

Level

2

Chapter 1 – Introduction to IT Key Skills

Objectives

- ❑ To learn what is involved in gaining the Key Skills in Information Technology certificate
- ❑ To understand the type of evidence that should be collected and included in a portfolio
- ❑ To examine the sheets required for the Key Skills log book to be included in the portfolio

1.1 The Key Skills units

The QCA specifications for the Key Skills units in Information Technology at Levels 2 and 3 are shown in the Appendix.

Each unit comprises two sections:

- ❑ **Part A** explains what you need to know.
- ❑ **Part B** identifies what you must do.

1.2 Assessment

You will be assessed through a combination of internal portfolio evidence (described in Part B above) and external assessment (a test of the skills identified in Part A above).

When your portfolio of evidence has been assessed by your teacher or lecturer (and possibly moderated by the awarding body) and you have passed the test, you will receive an IT Key Skills certificate.

1.3 How this book can help you

The underpinning skills and knowledge that you need to acquire for Part A are covered by Chapters 2-12. Sample test questions are given at the end of each chapter where appropriate.

Working through the sample activities in each chapter and then completing similar examples will provide you with the evidence required for your portfolio (Part B of the specification.) At the end of each chapter we show how those activities meet the requirements of the specification. Advice is also given on what to include in your folder – tick the items off in the list provided to ensure that you do not discard some useful evidence by mistake. Sample recording sheets are provided at www.payne-gallway.co.uk/ksit – these can be photocopied and included in your portfolio, to be completed as you work on your chosen activities.

It may not be necessary to cover everything in the book. Chapters 2 to 7 cover the skills and evidence required for Level 2. If you are working at this level you may feel it unnecessary to move on to the Level 3 chapters - unless you become particularly riveted by some piece of software! If you are working towards the level 3 qualification then you need to complete the Level 2 chapters (much of which may already be familiar to you) and then move on to cover the Level 3 chapters.

1.4 Preparing for the Test

Ensure that you have covered the skills and knowledge in all of the chapters appropriate for your level of study. Even if you do not intend to use similar activities as evidence in your portfolio, you could be asked a question on them in the test. Try the sample questions as you work through each chapter. When you have covered all the topics you should attempt the sample tests available on the web site of either your examining body or QCA, which will provide further practice in the type of questions you are likely to encounter. The tests that you take as part of the assessment for the Key Skills qualification will be externally set by QCA. They are designed to enable you to show what you know about IT and how you can apply the knowledge you have gained for Part A to an appropriate task.

It is likely that your awarding body will offer more than one opportunity throughout the year for you to sit the test. Your school or college will notify you of the date(s).

Level 2

The test will be of 1 hour's duration. You will be asked to answer up to 40 compulsory questions, some or all of which will be multiple-choice. The questions will be based around a number of common themes linked to common, everyday situations.

Level 3

This test will be of 1.5 hour's duration. It will comprise tasks to be completed at a computer.

1.5 Collecting your evidence

You can select a combination of activities to include in your portfolio of evidence. You must have evidence that you can do all the tasks listed in the bullet points in Part B of the specification (shown in the Appendix).

There may be opportunities to develop and generate evidence in your main course of study. You will be supplied with either **Signposting** or **Keys to Attainment** depending on what you are studying (e.g. 'A'/'AS' Levels, Advanced Vocational Certificate of Education, Intermediate GNVQ etc.). If your school or college recommends you use this total or partially integrated approach you will still need to use the skills described in Chapters 2-12 to produce the evidence.

If your school or college is providing you with separate Key Skills sessions in which to produce evidence, you should learn the skills and knowledge given in the chapters and then produce evidence from everyday, 'real' examples if you can (they always work better than imaginary, 'simulated' situations). Think of examples from home, your part-time job or a club you belong to, for example.

Level 2

At this level you need to carry out at least two activities which include tasks for each bullet point in Part B IT2.1, IT2.2 and IT2.3.

Overall, through these two or more activities you must:

♦ include one IT-based information source and one non-IT based information source

♦ include at least one example of **text**, one example of **images** and one example of **numbers**

♦ present evidence of the purposeful use of e-mail.

Level 3

At level 3 you must plan and carry through a number of different tasks, one of which must be a major task which covers each bullet point in all components i.e. IT3.1, IT3.2, and IT3.3. Each component must be covered at least twice and IT3.3 must be covered for at least **two different audiences.**

Overall, through these activities you must:

♦ include at least one IT-based information source and one non-IT based information source

♦ include at least one example of **text**, one example of **images** and one example of **numbers**

♦ use one example of combined information such as text and number, or image and number or text and image

♦ present evidence of sending and receiving e-mail; one of these e-mails must have an attachment related to the task.

Note that at both levels you are asked to provide **sufficient** evidence as specified in Part B of the specification. Do not include too much evidence; it will just make it more difficult for the assessor or moderator to identify evidence for a particular component.

1.6 Other Key Skills signposting

At the end of the chapters in this book (where appropriate) we have signposted how the work you have completed could be used as evidence for other Key Skills. You may have just one portfolio for all the Key Skills units or separate portfolios, in which case you will have to cross-reference the evidence in your Key Skills log book.

1.7 Types of evidence

The evidence that you should collect for each activity is listed at the end of the chapters. You will see that the type of evidence can vary. For example, it could include some of the following:

♦ Plans of the work you intend to undertake, perhaps with some key 'milestone' dates identified. It is recommended that you record these details on a separate sheet similar to the sample **Planning record sheet** provided at www.payne-gallway.co.uk/ksit.

♦ A written description of the activity.

♦ Printouts from the Internet as evidence of research sources.

♦ Notes on other research sources (for example, book/journal titles etc.). It is recommended that you record these details on a separate sheet similar to the sample **Information Seeking record sheet** provided at www.payne-gallway.co.uk/ksit.

♦ Notes on how you completed tasks.

♦ Draft printouts, annotated to describe techniques you have used.

♦ Draft printouts, annotated to show corrections that were required.

♦ Screenshots of your work in progress (for example, if you want evidence that you have spell-checked a document, take a screenshot with the spell-check dialogue box showing – details of how to take screenshots are given in Chapter 11).

♦ Final printouts of documents.

♦ A written, signed record from your assessor of how you completed the work.

If producing certain types of evidence is difficult for you because of disability or for some other reason, you may be able to produce evidence in a different way. For example, you could discuss with your tutor the use of audio or video tape evidence or photographic evidence.

An extract from a sample portfolio can be downloaded from the Payne-Gallway web site. The evidence is similar to that which may have been produced to complete the Desk Top Publishing activity in Chapter 12.

1.8   Your IT Key Skills Log Book

You should be given some form of IT Key Skills log book (a sample is provided at www.payne-gallway.co.uk/ksit – it is not so much a 'book' as a collection of sheets to put in your portfolio). Most examining bodies supply their own version of these recording sheets. These allow you to record the context of evidence that you have generated and its exact location in your folder. They should also record the date the work was assessed and by whom.

Every time you produce work for your IT Key Skills portfolio you should get into the routine of doing the following:

- Use the table in the paragraph **Evidence for your portfolio** at the end of the appropriate chapter as a checklist of the evidence you are collecting for that activity.

- Put the piece of work into your portfolio and number it (e.g. in the top right-hand corner).

- Find the appropriate **KEY SKILLS LOG BOOK COMPONENT SHEET** (e.g. Component IT2.1, etc.). Fill in the column **HOW MET** against the appropriate Assessment Criteria (bullet point). (Use the paragraph **Relating this chapter to the specification** near the end of the appropriate chapter to help you to do this.)

- Date it and ask your assessor to sign it.

- In your **KEY SKILLS LOG BOOK UNIT SUMMARY** record the number you have assigned the piece of work against the appropriate Key Skills requirement.

Your teacher/lecturer should assess your progress at regular intervals. Ensure they sign and date your log book whenever they assess a piece of work. In this way you will be able to monitor how you are progressing with the qualification.

1.9   Additional web site resources

Several activities in this book require text or image files to complete the activities. Sample files are available from the web site page www.payne-gallway.co.uk/ksit where indicated. Chapter 6 offers advice on how to download files.

Chapter 2 – Introduction to Windows

Objectives

- ❑ To recognise objects on the Windows XP desktop and to manipulate windows
- ❑ To create and name new folders to organise work efficiently and logically
- ❑ To understand the importance of making backups
- ❑ To move, copy, rename and delete files and folders
- ❑ To understand the use of the Recycle Bin
- ❑ To find a file or folder using searches specifying various criteria

2.1   Exploring the desktop

When you switch your computer on, you will probably be asked to log on by entering a user name and password. If no user name and password has been set, you can just press **Enter**, otherwise you must enter the user name and correct password.

You will then see the **Desktop** which will be similar to that shown in Figure 2.1.

Program icons. Double-click an icon to run the program represented by the icon.

*The **Start** menu. Click to display a list of programs to select from. You also click **Start** when you want to shut down your computer.*

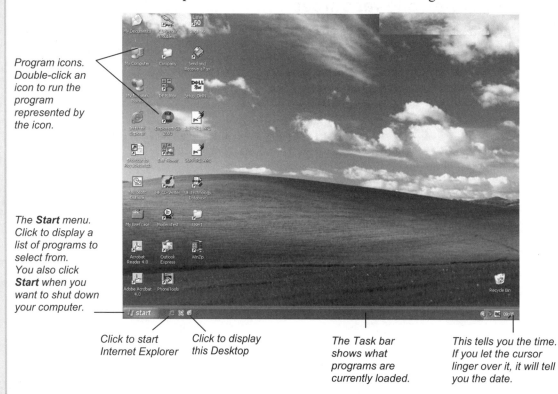

Click to start Internet Explorer

Click to display this Desktop

The Task bar shows what programs are currently loaded.

This tells you the time. If you let the cursor linger over it, it will tell you the date.

Figure 2.1: The Windows XP desktop

2.2 Shutting down the computer

You probably don't want to do this right now. But just make a mental note – don't ever just switch the computer off and walk away. Follow the rules set by the boys and girls in white shirts and dark suits at Microsoft.

- Save any files that you have been working on and want to keep.
- Close down any programs that are currently running.
- Remove your disk from the **A:** drive if you have been using one.
- Click **Start** at the bottom left of the screen and select **Turn Off Computer**.
- The following screen appears. Click the **Turn Off** option.
- Wait till the screen goes blank and then switch the screen off.

Figure 2.2: Shutting down the computer

2.3 Manipulating windows

Sizing windows

- Display the Desktop on your screen if it is not already displayed. (You can do this by clicking the **Desktop** icon on the Taskbar at the bottom of your screen – see Figure 2.1.)
- Double-click the icon for **My Computer**. The My Computer window will appear.
- Reduce its size by clicking the **Restore Down** icon – this is the middle one of the three icons in the top right-hand corner of the window.
- You can drag the Title bar of the window to position the window anywhere on the screen.
- Make the window smaller by dragging a corner in towards the centre. It will look something like Figure 2.3 – although you may be displaying a different view of the icons. You will learn in a minute how to change the view.

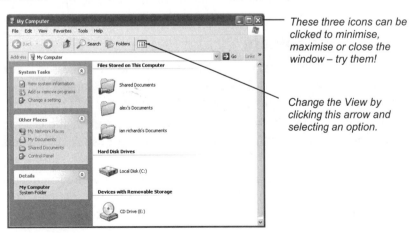

These three icons can be clicked to minimise, maximise or close the window – try them!

Change the View by clicking this arrow and selecting an option.

Figure 2.3: The resized My Computer window

Precisely what use is this window? Well, by clicking on the icon for the **C:** drive you can see how much disk space you have free. By clicking **Control Panel** on the left you can display the Control Panel window, from which you can change practically all the settings on your computer.

- Double-click the **Control Panel** icon. The Control Panel window appears.

- Double-click the **Date/Time** icon. If your computer's clock is showing the wrong time you can put it right here.

Figure 2.4: The desktop with several windows open

Activating, minimising, maximising and closing a window

The active window has a blue Title bar. You can bring a window to the front and make it active simply by clicking in it.

- Resize the Control Panel window so that it is just big enough for all the icons to be visible.

- Click the My Computer window to make it active.

- Click the **Minimize** icon in the top left-hand corner. This reduces the window to a button in the task bar at the bottom of the screen.

- Click the **My Computer** button on the task bar, and the window will return to its original size.

- Click the **Maximize** icon to maximize the window.

- Click the **Close** icon to close the window.

- Close the Control Panel window. Now there should be no open windows on the desktop.

2.4 Files and folders

All the documents you create on your PC, such as a word-processed letter, a spreadsheet, a database or a graphic, are referred to as **files**. A file could be for example a piece of Clip Art, a game, a web page, a spreadsheet, or a utility program to zip (compress) a file or format a disk.

File names can be up to 255 characters long, so it is a good idea to give your files meaningful names so that you can easily find them again. You can't use the characters * | \ < > ? / " : in a filename.

File names are given *extensions* (a dot followed by usually three characters) to help identify what type of file they are. For example, documents created in Word are given the extension **.doc**, spreadsheets created in Excel **.xls**, databases created in Access **.mdb**.

As time goes by you will find you have hundreds, probably even thousands, of files stored on your hard drive. It is therefore extremely important to keep your work organised so that you can easily find that letter you wrote six months ago demanding a refund on the box of cereal that was missing the football player inside it.

In a manual business system, you would keep your correspondence, supplier records, customer records, budgets and so on in a filing cabinet. Maybe you would have one drawer for Suppliers, one for Customers, one for Overseas Sales, one for Accounts, etc. Within each Supplier folder, you might keep several past orders and invoices. Within each Customer folder there might be several letters, contracts, etc.

You use a very similar system on a computer.

For example, suppose you are going to use your computer for the following tasks:

Key Skills in Communication
Key Skills in Application of Number
Key Skills in IT
Geography Notes
Business Studies Notes
Letters to friends
Timetable of lessons
Holiday budget plan
CV
Letters of application for various jobs
Advertisement for clapped-out old Ford Fiesta
Games downloaded from the Internet

(You can probably think of dozens of other things you save on your computer.)

Step 1: Recognise that some of the above items are categories which need to be folders, and others are just single documents. For example within **Key Skills in IT** you are probably going to store many different types of document as you build up your portfolio. You will need a folder called, for example, **KSIT**.

Step 2: Within this folder you probably need subfolders for each project in your portfolio. Suppose your first project is to produce leaflets and a budget for a group holiday or trip. You could set up a subfolder within **KSIT** called **Holiday Project**.

You could organise the above list as follows (though there are many other ways of doing it!).

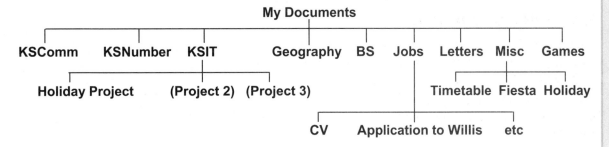

Figure 2.5: Organising work into folders and subfolders

To create these folders and subfolders, move them around, delete them and rename them, you will use **Windows Explorer**.

2.5 Introducing Windows Explorer

When the Windows operating system is first loaded onto your computer (probably before you even take it out of the box) it names each of your drives as shown in Figure 2.3. The floppy drive is named **A:**, the hard drive **C:**, the Zip drive if you have one is probably **D:**, the CD drive **E:** and so on. On a network, the hard drive is usually partitioned (divided up) into several 'logical drives' called **F:**, **G:**, **H:** etc.

On the **C:** drive Windows sets up a number of folders, and every time you load on new software such as Word, Excel and Access another collection of new folders is created and files put into them. Some of these folders contain program modules, some contain collections of Clip Art, some contain drivers to make your printer and other devices work correctly.

One very important folder that is automatically set up for you is called **My Documents**. This is where Windows expects you to create your own subfolders to store your work. You can create folders outside **My Documents** too if you want to. The important thing is to plan how you are going to organise all the work you do on your computer and set up folders and subfolders accordingly.

Figure 2.6 below shows a small part of the directory structure (i.e. the system of folders and subfolders) set up on my computer. You can probably find several things to criticise about my organisational abilities!

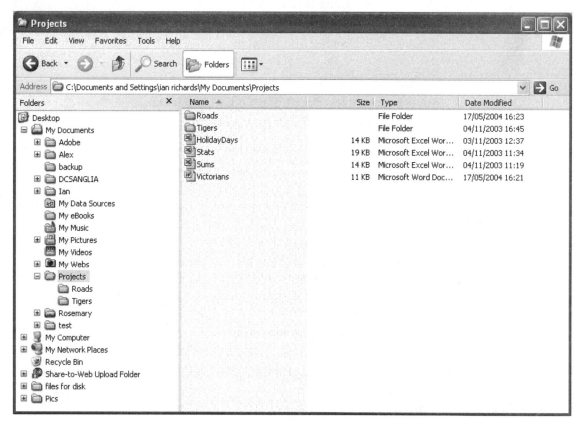

Figure 2.6: A typical Windows Explorer Screen

Changing the view

The list of folders and files in the right-hand window is shown in **Details** view. You can change this.

- Go to the Desktop by clicking the Desktop icon near the **Start** button at the bottom right of your screen or by right-clicking in the Task bar and selecting **Show the Desktop**.

- Open Windows Explorer by right-clicking the **Start** button and selecting **Explore**.

- Look in the left-hand pane and find the **My Documents** folder. Click it to open it, and the contents will be displayed in the right-hand pane.

My Documents will most likely contain some subfolders and some files. The **Views** button on the toolbar allows you to view the contents in different formats

- Click the arrow next to the Views button on the toolbar.

- Try out the different views.

Figure 2.7 below shows the right-hand pane in Icon view. Of course, you will not have the same folders or documents on your screen.

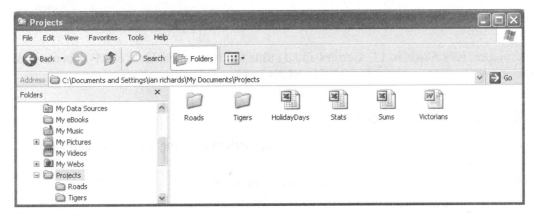

Figure 2.7: Contents of Projects folder in Icon view

Note that in the left-hand pane, the **Projects** folder (currently selected) has a picture of an open folder next to it. This tells you that all the subfolders and files in the right-hand pane are contained in **Projects**. You can also see the subfolders listed in the left-hand pane underneath **Projects**.

Beside the open folder symbol next to **Projects** is a little box containing a minus sign. If you click that, you will no longer see the subfolders and documents contained in **Projects** in the left-hand pane.

- Check what symbol is next to your **My Documents** folder. If it is a plus (+) sign, you will not see any subfolders or files contained in **My Documents**, in the left-hand pane.

- Click the symbol. It changes to a minus (–) sign, and the subfolders become visible. The right-hand pane does not change.

- If there are some subfolders showing a plus sign, you can click the plus sign to display their contents in the left-hand pane.

The contents of the **Tigers** subfolder shown in Figure 2.7 can be displayed either by clicking the **Tigers** folder icon in the left-hand pane, or double-clicking the **Tigers** folder icon in the right-hand pane.

If you double-click one of the *documents* in the right-hand pane, it will open in the appropriate software package (shown by the icon). For example if you click **Victorians.doc**, Word will start up and the document will open. If you double-click **Stats.xls**, Excel will start up with this spreadsheet.

In this task you will first create new folders in a structure like this:

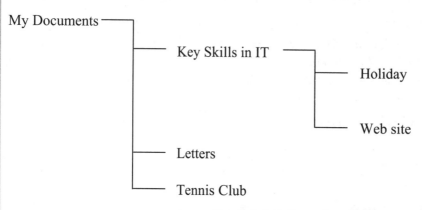

Figure 2.8: A directory structure

In this structure, **Key Skills in IT**, **Letters** and **Tennis Club** are subfolders of **My Documents**, and **Holiday** and **Web site** are subfolders of **Key Skills in IT**.

2.6   Creating a new folder

- Open Windows Explorer if it is not already open, by right-clicking the **Start** button and selecting **Explore**.

You can also access Windows Explorer from **My Computer**:

- Click **Start**, **My Computer.**
- Select **Tools**, **Folder Options** from the menu and click the **General** tab.
- Select the option **Windows classic folders** and click **OK**.
- Click the **Folders** button on the toolbar.

You should now see the directory structure displayed as shown in Figures 2.6 or 2.7 (depending on the view selected).

- Click on the **My Documents** folder in the left-hand pane.
- Click the **View** button on the toolbar and select **Details**.
- With **My Documents** selected, click **File**, **New**, **Folder** on the menu bar. At the bottom of the list of files and folders a new folder with the name **New Folder** appears. Type the name *Key Skills in IT* over this and press **Enter**. There! You have created a new folder.
- With **My Documents** selected, click **File**, **New**, **Folder** on the menu bar again. This time, name the new folder *Letters*.
- Create the third folder, **Tennis Club**.
- In the left-hand pane, make sure that all the subfolders of My Documents are showing. Select **Key Skills in IT** in this pane, and select **File**, **New**, **Folder** again. This time, the new subfolder (name it *Holiday*) will be contained in **Key Skills in IT**.
- Create the last subfolder, **Web site**.
- Minimise the Explorer window by clicking the **Minimize** icon in the top right-hand corner.

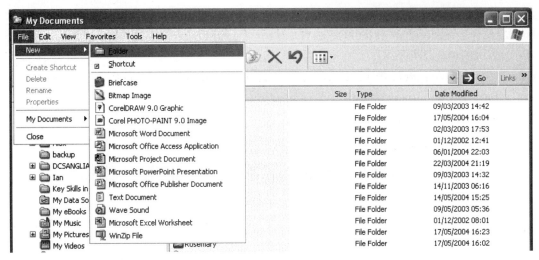

Figure 2.9: Creating a new folder

2.7   Saving a document in a folder

- Open Word by double-clicking the Word icon on the desktop, or by clicking **Start**, **Programs**, **Microsoft Word**.

- Write a couple of lines of a letter – anything will do. "Dear John, Come back, all is forgiven…"

- From the menu select **File**, **Save As**.

Word may select **My Documents** as the default folder for your documents, or it may select a different folder that has previously been set as the default.

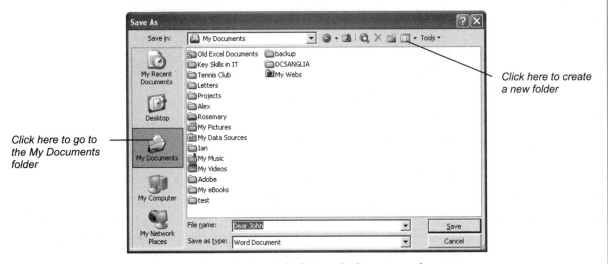

Figure 2.10: Selecting a folder in which to save a document

- To get to the **My Documents** folder, click **My Documents** on the left of the screen.

- Scroll down if necessary to find the **Letters** folder and double-click it.

- The document is automatically named the same as the first few words. You may want to give it a more meaningful name including possibly the date that you wrote the letter. Click **Save.**

- Note that you can create a new folder in this window. You don't have to do it in Explorer.

- Without closing the first document, create a second letter in Word. Select **File**, **New** from the menu and type a second short letter, e.g. "Dear Sir, I write to say how disgusted I am with the quality of your chocolates…"

- Save it in the Letters folder as Disgusted.

- Open a third new document and just type a heading "*Holiday Project*".

- Click **File**, **Save** to save the document.

- You need to go up one level of folder. Click the button as shown in Figure 2.11.

Figure 2.11: Moving up one level of folder

- This will take you to the **My Documents** folder. Double-click the **Key Skills in IT** folder to save this document in that folder, leaving the default document name **Holiday Project**.

- Notice that all the document names are listed in the Task bar at the bottom of the screen. You can click on any of them to make that the active document.

Figure 2.12: The documents appear minimised in the Taskbar

- Close all three Word documents, and close Word to return to Windows Explorer.

2.8 Moving documents and folders

- Maximise Explorer.

- Find the **Letters** folder in the left-hand window and click it. The two document names appear in the right-hand window. We will move **Disgusted** into the **Tennis Club** folder.

- Make sure the **Tennis Club** folder is visible in the left-hand window.

- Click and drag the document **Disgusted** from the right-hand pane onto the folder **Tennis Club** in the left-hand pane. It disappears from the right-hand pane and if you click the **Tennis Club** folder, you will find it has moved.

- If Drag and Drop is not convenient, you can use Cut and Paste. Move the document back into the letters folder, using Cut and Paste from the **Edit** menu. Select the document, click **Edit**, **Cut**. Then select the **Letters** folder and select **Edit**, **Paste**.

- Use either of these methods to move **Holiday Project** from the **Key Skills in IT** folder into the **Letters** folder.

Selecting several documents

If you want to move several documents into a different folder, you can select them all and move them in one operation.

- To select non-consecutive documents, select the first document you wish to move and hold down **Ctrl** while you select another one, say the third document. This selects just the first and third documents. You could now drag them to a different location.

- To select a list of consecutive documents, select the first one and then hold down **Shift** while you select the last one. This selects the whole list.

- Practise moving your documents between folders.

- You can move folders to different locations too. Try moving the **Letters** folder so that it becomes a subfolder of **Tennis Club**.

2.9 Making backups

Making backups is an absolutely crucial task when you do any work on a computer that you don't want to lose. Windows XP has extremely sophisticated Backup facilities, but it will probably be sufficient for you to work out a simple backup strategy and be sure you stick to it. There are several reasons for making backups. For example:

- You could save your work in class on a floppy disk and then accidentally leave it in the machine. You will probably never see it again.

- The floppy disk could become unreadable if it becomes overheated, bent, or simply old.

- Your document could become corrupted because you did something wrong, or the system crashed, and you want to revert to an earlier version.

- Your hard disk could crash, and everything on it will be lost.

- Your computer could be stolen, especially if you use a laptop.

You can probably think of other potential disasters. Your backup strategy should be comprehensive enough to guard against any possible loss, either through accident, carelessness or catastrophe.

- If you work on floppy disks, always have two spare floppy disks and save your work onto your working disk and one of the backup disks. Leave one safe at home. Label all three disks very carefully and alternate the two backup disks.

- If you work on a hard drive, create a backup folder on the hard drive and copy your work into it at the end of a session. This will not protect against a hard disk crash so copy your work onto a floppy disk or zip disk every so often. Label it carefully and store it somewhere safely.

Copying folders and files

We will practise making backups.

- Create a new folder in the **My Documents** folder called **Project Backup**.

- Now we want to copy the **Key Skills in IT** folder, together with all its contents, into the **Project Backup** folder. To do this you can either use **Copy** and **Paste** from the **Edit** menu, or you can hold down the **Ctrl** key while you drag and drop.

- Use one of the above methods to copy it into the backup folder.

Renaming folders and files

If the backup folder and files have exactly the same names as the originals, it is easy to open a backup document by mistake and then find you have not been working with the latest version. To avoid this happening you can rename the folders and documents.

- Select the **Key Skills in IT** folder in the **Project Backup** folder.

- Right-click it and select **Rename**. The name will be highlighted ready for you to type a new name. Click at the end of the name and type *(Backup)* to give it the name **Key Skills in IT (Backup)**. Press **Enter**.

> **Note:**   If you make a mistake while changing a name, simply press **Escape** to cancel the process.

2.10 Searching for files

As you create more and more files and folders over a period of months and years, it can be hard to remember where you put them and what they are called, however well organised you are. Windows XP has a powerful tool called the **Search Companion** to help you locate files and folders anywhere on your computer. You can search using different criteria such as just a few letters of the file name, date last modified etc.

For example, you can look for all Word documents with **Key** in the title that were created in the last 3 months.

- To launch the Search Companion, click the **Search** button on the Standard Buttons toolbar in Windows Explorer. Alternatively, from the **Start** menu in the bottom left of the screen, select **Search**.

The Search Companion opens as shown on the left of Figure 2.13.

 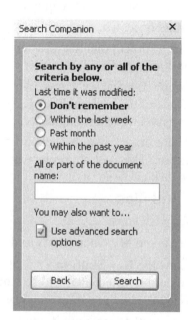

Figure 2.13: The Search Companion in Windows Explorer

- Click on **Documents** in the first window and then specify when the document was last modified in the next window.

- To search for all files and folders containing the word **Key**, type *KEY** into the box (it does not matter whether you use uppercase or lowercase letters.)

The Search results will be shown in the right-hand pane. You can double-click a document name to open it.

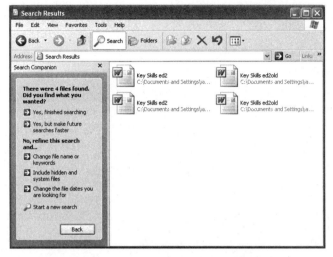

Figure 2.14: Search results displayed

- Have a look at some of the **Advanced Search Options** (see Figure 2.13) to perform more complex searches.

- Close the Search Companion by clicking the **Close** icon in its top right-hand corner.

- Experiment with the other buttons on the toolbar; for example, clicking the **Folders** button and selecting **My Documents** in the Address list box will return you to the more familiar screen in Windows Explorer.

2.11 Deleting documents and folders

That's enough practice on manipulating folders and files! Now we'll delete the whole lot.

- Select the **My Documents** folder so that all the subfolders and documents are shown in the right-hand pane.

- Select the folders you created in this chapter (careful you select the right ones!) You can select them all by holding down **Ctrl** while you click each one. (See Figure 2.15).

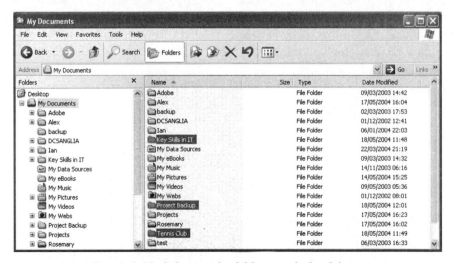

Figure 2.15: Selecting the folders ready for deletion

- Press the **Delete** key on the keyboard. Gone!

> **Note:** If you change your mind about a deletion or a rename, you can undo it by selecting **Undo Delete** or **Undo Rename** from the **Edit** menu.

2.12 The Recycle Bin

Where do files and folders go when you have deleted them? They go into a special folder called the **Recycle Bin**. This means that if you later decide that you want to retrieve the files or folders, you can move them out of the Recycle Bin back into **My Documents**.

The Recycle Bin by default can occupy up to 10% of the space on your hard drive. When it becomes completely full, Windows starts automatically deleting files, beginning with the oldest. If you are short of space, you can delete files from the Recycle Bin just as you can from any other folder. You can delete selected files and folders, or empty the whole bin in one go by right-clicking the **Recycle Bin** icon on the desktop and selecting **Empty Recycle Bin** from the shortcut menu.

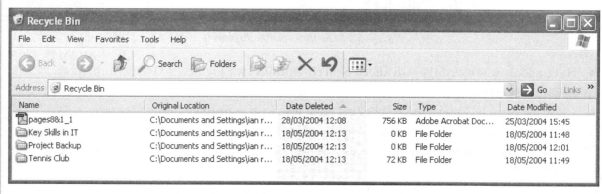

Figure 2.16: Folders and files in the Recycle Bin

> **Note:** On some school or college networks the Recycle Bin may be disabled, so when you delete a file, it really is deleted – the same applies to files on a floppy disk.

2.13 Summary

This chapter has covered some of the background knowledge that you need to work effectively when you use a PC. It is essential to know how to keep your work well organised in files and folders and to be able to find, move, copy or delete files. The importance of making regular backups of your work cannot be over-emphasised.

For example, at Level 3 you are required to demonstrate that your work is saved appropriately (e.g. using suitable folders/directories and file names, and avoiding loss). This is discussed further in Chapter 7.

2.14 Sample questions

Task 1

1. Open Windows Explorer, create a new folder in **My Documents** and name it **ITwork**.
2. Open Microsoft Word and create a new blank document, name it **WPone** and save it in the folder called **ITwork**.
3. Open Microsoft Excel and create a new blank workbook, name it **SSone** and save it in the folder **ITwork**.
4. Return to Windows Explorer and create two new folders within **ITwork** called **WPwork** and **SSwork**.
5. Copy the file **WPone** into the folder **WPwork**.
6. Move the file **SSone** into the folder **SSwork**.
7. Delete the copy of the file **WPone** in the folder **ITwork**.
8. Rename the folder **ITwork** as **Workfiles**.
9. Sketch a block diagram to show the file structure you have created.

Task 2

1. Where would you change the system date/time settings?
   A   The Recycle bin
   B   The Tools menu
   C   A spreadsheet package
   D   The control panel

2. What file extension is given to Word documents?
   A   .xls
   B   .doc
   C   .ppt
   D   .mdb

3. What letter is the floppy disk drive normally assigned?
   A   E:\
   B   C:\
   C   A:\
   D   Z:\

4. In Windows Explorer which key would you hold down to select non-consecutive files?
   A   Shift
   B   Ctrl
   C   Alt
   D   Caps Lock

5. Where would you find the command to create a new folder in Windows Explorer?
   A   The File menu
   B   The Go menu
   C   The Tools menu
   D   The View menu

6. The best way to ensure that a new word processing document is not lost is to:
   A   Create a backup file
   B   Create a hard copy
   C   Create a new empty file
   D   Put it in the Recycle Bin

Chapter 3 – Introduction to Word Processing

Objectives

- ❏ To use an appropriate layout, styles and formatting in a document produced for a particular purpose
- ❏ To edit a document using cut and paste, spell-checking, drag and drop, find and replace
- ❏ To use WordArt, insert Clip Art, and insert a picture from an Internet site
- ❏ To change margins and tab settings
- ❏ To use borders and shading
- ❏ To use bulleted and numbered lists
- ❏ To insert a table into a word-processed document
- ❏ To apply the skills learned to other projects and to learn how to gather appropriate evidence for a portfolio

Sample task: Create a brochure advertising holiday cottages for rent

In this task you will use Microsoft Word to create a well-laid out paragraph or two describing one of the cottages that is rented out in the Scottish Highlands by a small family business. The brochure will be illustrated with pictures.

3.1   Finding the information for your brochure

Before you begin to use the word processing software to produce your brochure you must take the time to find some relevant information to include in it. For example the information for this type of holiday brochure could be found on the Internet. There are many web sites that are available to make holiday bookings – use one of the search engines described in Chapter 6 to search for these sites. You will find that they generally include descriptions of the holidays on offer. Alternatively, drop in at your local travel agents and ask if they have any old brochures that you could have. Again these provide the type of information that you could base your brochure on.

You could also write the text from your first-hand experiences on holiday and scan in some of your own photographs.

Remember to record the sources of your information and why you chose them on an Information Seeking record sheet (a sample is provided at www.payne-gallway.co.uk/ksit).

It is also a good idea to draw some rough sketches (by hand) of the brochure layout before you begin on the computer.

For this sample activity you are provided with some text and you will use Clip Art and photographs imported from the Internet.

3.2 Opening Word and displaying selected menus

- Load Word by double-clicking the Word icon or clicking the **Start** menu and selecting **Programs**, **Microsoft Word**.

The Word opening screen appears as shown below:

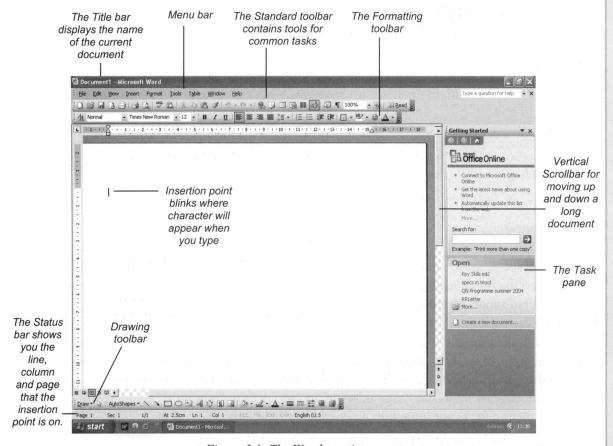

Figure 3.1: The Word opening screen

A new document opens automatically with the name **Document1**, ready for you to start typing.

- Spend a few minutes looking at the options available on the toolbars.

On the **Standard toolbar** there are buttons to start a new file, open an existing file, save a file and so on. If you let the pointer linger for a few seconds over a button, a tool tip appears telling you what the button does.

Using tools on the **Formatting toolbar** you can change the style of text, choose a font and font size, and change the appearance of the text in many different ways.

The **Drawing toolbar** at the bottom of the screen may not be visible. You can display it at any time by clicking the **Drawing** icon or selecting **View, Toolbars, Drawing** from the menu bar. Using tools on this toolbar you can draw and colour simple shapes, insert text boxes or Clip Art, or use WordArt to create interesting text effects.

The **Task pane** opens and closes automatically depending on what you are doing. You can close the Task pane at any time by clicking the **Close** icon in its top right-hand corner.

You can display the Task pane at any time from the **View** menu. You can display any toolbar by selecting **View**, **Toolbars** and choosing one from the list.

3.3 Creating, saving, closing and reopening a document

When you create a formatted document with centred headings, and different size and style of fonts, you can either type the text first and then apply a style to each part of the text, or select a font size and style first and then start typing.

We will start by typing the text in without bothering about styles, and then apply formatting to make it look attractive.

- Type the following text. The style in the **Style** box should be set to **Normal**, **Times New Roman 11** or **12** point.

Holly Cottage
Farley
2-6 people
Car included

Holly cottage is set in an idyllic location overlooking a valley where deer roam freely right up to the boundary of the garden (don't leave the gate open!). Behind the house the heather-clad moors stretch towards lakes and mountain peaks, providing walks of unparalleled beauty.
The house has three double bedrooms, a comfortable living room with a cosy wood-burning stove, and a fully equipped kitchen. Guests will soon master the art of cooking on the coal-burning Aga in the colder months of the year, or can take the easy way out and use the electric oven. The cottage is set in an attractive garden with lawns, mature trees and a barbecue for those long summer evenings, when darkness does not fall until after 10 o'clock.
A four-wheel drive comes with the cottage so that you can make the most of your stay by visiting the dozens of beauty spots both inland and around the coast.
Inverness is a twenty-minute drive away and regular flights and trains provide easy access from any part of the country. Taxis are available to whisk you to Farley on arrival at either the airport or the station.

Figure 3.2: The unformatted text

- Select **File, Save** from the menu or click the **Save** button on the Standard toolbar. A window similar to the one shown in Figure 3.3 appears.

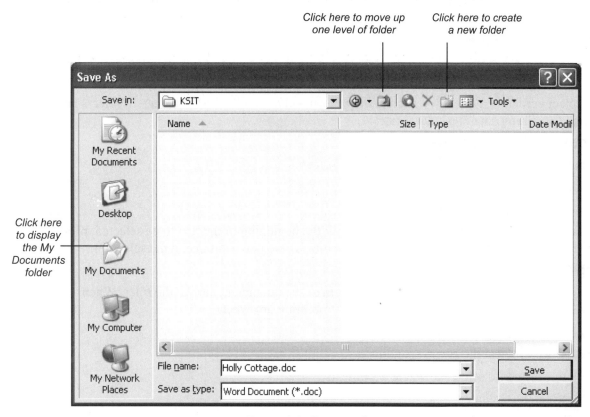

Figure 3.3: Saving a document

By default, documents are given a name based on the first few words in the document and saved in the **My Documents** folder.

- It would be a good idea to create a new folder to store all your Key Skills word processing tasks. Click the **New Folder** button to create a new folder within **My Documents** or wherever you normally store your work. Give the folder a name such as **KSIT**.

- Press the **Save** button when you have selected a suitable folder and file name.

Note that the new name appears in the Title bar.

- Close the document by clicking the black **Close Window** icon in the top right-hand corner of the document window. (Do not confuse this with the Word Close icon.)

Opening an existing document

- From the menu select **File**. A list of recently opened files appears at the bottom of the menu, and if yours is shown, you can click it to open it. If it is not shown, select **Open** to select it from the Open dialogue box. If the Task pane is visible and your document name is shown, you can click it to open the document.

- Open the document **Holly Cottage**.

3.4 Selecting text

There are several ways to select text. It is worth getting to know them, as these tips can save you hours of time.

Dragging the mouse

- You can drag the mouse across all the text that you want to select. If the selection goes over several lines just drag straight down from the selection point and then across on the last line.
- To select vertically, hold down **Alt** and drag down and across the text you want to select. This is useful for editing data in tabular form.

Selecting with the mouse

It's much quicker to click than drag. Try these shortcuts:

- Double-click a word to select it.
- Triple-click to select the paragraph.
- To select several paragraphs, place the cursor at the beginning of the text to be selected, press and hold down the **Shift** key, and click at the point where you want to end the selection.

Using the selection bar

The (invisible) selection bar is the left-hand margin of the document, next to the ruler. When you move the cursor into this area it changes to a right-pointing arrowhead.

- Click once to select the current line.
- Click twice to select the current paragraph.
- Click three times to select the whole document.
- To deselect the document, click in the right-hand margin.

Using the keyboard

- To select a single character use **Shift** and the right arrow key (or left arrow to select before the insertion point).
- To select a line at a time, press **Shift** and the down arrow key, or the up arrow key to select upwards.
- To select the entire document, press **Ctrl-A** (for All).

3.5 Formatting text

- Click in the selection bar to select the line **Holly Cottage**.
- Click the **Center** button to centre the text. (Note that you should NEVER try and centre text by using the Space bar.)
- Select a font size of **26** points.

Note that while there are literally thousands of different fonts (typefaces) available, they can be grouped into two basic categories – Serif and Sans Serif (literally, without serif.). Serifs are the tiny appendages projecting from a letter. In this book, the paragraph headings are in a 16-point Sans Serif font called **Arial**, and the text is in an 11-point serif font called **Times New Roman**.

Font size is commonly measured in points, with one point equal to $^1/_{72}$ of an inch.

- Select the next 3 lines and centre them.
- Make them bold and italic, using buttons on the Formatting toolbar.
- Change the font size of *Farley* to **18** point.
- Make the 2 lines underneath *Farley* Arial font.

- Select the rest of the text and click the **Justify** button. Justified text lines up on both the left and right margins, as opposed to left-justified or right-justified text, which line up on the left and right margins respectively.

- Select the entire text and click the Outside Border button to put a border around it. It should now look like Figure 3.4.

Holly Cottage
Farley
2-6 people
Car included

Holly cottage is set in an idyllic location overlooking a valley where deer roam freely right up to the boundary of the garden (don't leave the gate open!). Behind the house the moors stretch towards lakes and mountain peaks, providing walks of unparalleled beauty.

The house has three double bedrooms, a comfortable living room with a cosy wood-burning stove, and a fully equipped kitchen. Guests will soon master the art of cooking on the coal-burning Aga in the colder months of the year, or can take the easy way out and use the electric oven. The cottage is set in an attractive garden with lawns, mature trees and a barbecue for those long summer evenings, when darkness does not fall until after 10 o'clock.

A four-wheel drive comes with the cottage so that you can make the most of your stay by visiting the dozens of beauty spots both inland and around the coast.

Inverness is a twenty-minute drive away and regular flights and trains provide easy access from any part of the country. Taxis are available to whisk you to Farley on arrival at either the airport or the station.

Figure 3.4: Text justified and with formatted headings

Formatting paragraphs

We can add some space between each paragraph.

- Select all the text except the 4 lines of heading, and right-click the mouse. The following shortcut menu is displayed.

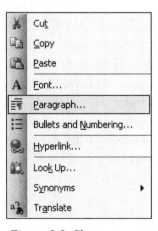

Figure 3.5: Shortcut menu

- Click **Paragraph** and the following dialogue box is displayed.

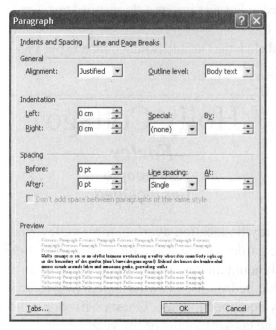

Figure 3.6: The Paragraph menu

- Click the Up arrow beside the **Spacing Before:** box. This sets the spacing to 6 points.
- Click **OK**. You will see that 6 points of extra space has been inserted before each paragraph.

Take a look at the other options in this dialogue box. Several types of indents are available: you can specify indentations from the left or the right of selected text and also some special indents. These include a **first line** indent which, as you may have guessed, indents the first line only and a **hanging** indent, which indents all of the paragraph text *except* for the first line. Hanging indents are most useful in numbered and bulleted lists, where the numbers or bullets line up at the left margin and the rest of the text is indented. In the same dialogue box you can also specify line spacing – normally **Single** or **Double**.

3.6   Editing a document

Cut and paste

Suppose you now decide to switch the second and third paragraphs. There are two easy ways to do this: **cut and paste**, or **drag and drop**. Try cut and paste first.

- Drag down the left-hand margin to select the paragraph beginning 'The house has three double bedrooms…' (or triple-click anywhere in the paragraph.)
- Click the **Cut** button on the toolbar or select **Edit, Cut** from the menu. This puts the text into a special area of memory called the **Clipboard**.

- Move the pointer to the beginning of the paragraph starting 'Inverness is a twenty-minute drive away…' and click the **Paste** button or select **Edit, Paste** from the menu. The paragraph that you cut will be inserted just before this one.

Drag and drop

This is an even quicker way of moving text around.

- Select the same paragraph again.

- With the pointer somewhere in the paragraph, click and hold down the left mouse button while you drag the insertion point back to its original location so that the paragraphs are restored to their original order.

Find and Replace

Suppose you want to replace **Holly** with **Oak** throughout the text.

- Move the insertion point to the top of the document.

- From the menu select **Edit, Replace**.

- In the dialogue box, type *Holly* in the **Find What:** box, and *Oak* in the **Replace with:** box.

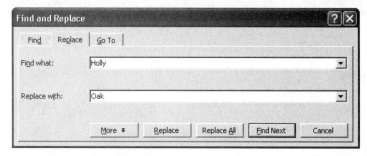

Figure 3.7: Finding and replacing text

- You can either click **Replace All**, or click **Find Next** and then **Replace** to replace each occurrence one at a time. This is safer as replacing text can sometimes have unexpected consequences. For example if you decided to replace a name *Sam* with *Harry* throughout a piece of text, words such as *same*, *sample* and *Samantha* would be changed to *harrye*, *harryple* and *Harryantha*.

- Click **More** to check out the options that are available. Then select a way to replace **Holly** with **Oak** and go ahead.

- Now try out the **Undo** button to undo both replacements.

Using the spell-checker

- Move the insertion point to the top of the document.

- Click the **Spelling and Grammar** button.

- If you have spelt everything correctly the only word that is likely to be queried is **Aga**. Word offers you several alternative spellings but you can click **Ignore All** to leave this word as it is. Correct any other misspellings in your document.

Moving outside the bordered text

One problem you may encounter at this point is that you can't go to a new line outside the bordered text. If so, simply double-click in the blank area (this feature is called **Click and Type**). Alternatively, click the **Outside Border** button to get rid of the border, press **Enter** to go to a new line and then replace the border around the text, but not around your new blank line.

- As we don't really want the border anyway, leave the text without a border.

Inserting a page break

- With the insertion point at the end of the document, select **Insert, Break... Page Break** from the menu. A quick way to insert a page break is to press **Ctrl-Enter**.

3.7 Inserting graphics

Inserting a scanned photograph

You may have a photograph of your own that you have scanned and want to insert into a document, or you may have found one on a CD or on the Internet that you can insert without infringing copyright. We will insert a scanned photograph into the holiday brochure.

- In the document **Holly Cottage.doc** place the insertion point under the text, and press **Enter** to leave a blank line.

- From the menu select **Insert, Picture, From File**.

- A dialogue box appears. You need to have a picture ready to insert. The one in the screenshot below is saved as **moorland.tif** and can be downloaded from www.payne-gallway.co.uk/ksit (see Chapter 6 for details on downloading files).

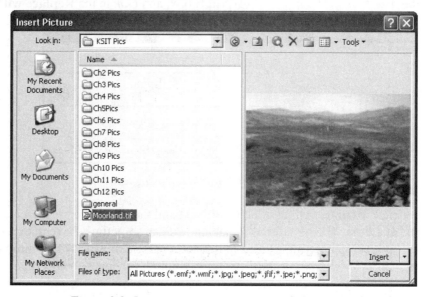

Figure 3.8: Inserting a picture or scanned photograph

- Click **OK**. The picture will be inserted.

Inserting Clip Art

Next we will insert a picture of a stag. You can look for one in the Clip Art gallery supplied with Word, but if there is nothing suitable, you can search the much more extensive online gallery.

- Place the insertion point at the end of the first paragraph, after the word 'beauty'.

- From the menu select **Insert, Picture, Clip Art**.

- In the Insert Clip Art Task pane, if you have an Internet connection, select **Clip art on Office Online**.

- Internet Explorer starts up. You will be connected to http://office.microsoft.com/clipart/default.asp. In the **Search for:** box, type *deer*. Click **Go**.

- A range of suitable pictures appears as shown in Figure 3.9. Select one of them by clicking in the box underneath it.

Figure 3.9: Downloading the stag picture

- Click **Download** in the left-hand window and follow the instructions on the next few screens.
- The picture will be automatically inserted into the Clip Organizer.

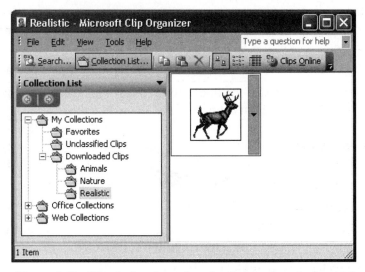

Figure 3.10: Clip Art has been downloaded ready to be inserted

- Return to the Insert Clip art Task pane and search for *deer*. When your new clip is displayed click the arrow next to it and select **Insert**.

Selecting a Clip Art layout

The picture of the stag is inserted underneath the text. You may decide you want it, for example, to the right of the first paragraph.

- Right-click the picture and select **Format Picture**. A dialogue box is displayed. Click the **Layout** tab.

- Select **Square and Right** as shown in Figure 3.11, and click **OK**.

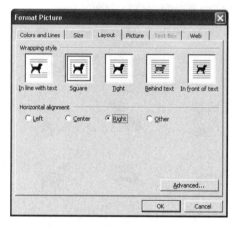

Figure 3.11: Positioning a picture

You can now drag the picture to the exact position you want it.

Sizing, moving and cropping an image

- Drag a corner handle to adjust the size. If you drag a side or top/bottom handle you will distort the picture.

- Experiment with other layouts such as **Tight and Right**. This makes the text wrap around the graphic.

- When the graphic is selected, you can use the cursor keys to make fine adjustments in position.

> **Note:** You drag a corner handle to **size** the image which means to change the size of the picture. **Cropping** an image means to cut off part of the image like this:

To crop the image:

- Click the image to select it.
- Display the Picture toolbar by selecting **View**, **Toolbars**, **Picture**.
- Click the **Crop** tool on the Picture toolbar.
- Drag the bottom handle around the picture upwards.
- Click the **Crop** tool again to turn it off.

Inserting a textbox

You can put a caption beside the photograph.

- Drag a corner handle to adjust the size of the photograph (see Figure 3.12)
- From the Drawing toolbar, select the **Text Box** tool.

- Drag out a box beside the Moorland photograph. Insert the text *The moors and mountains stretching into the distance behind Farley.*

> Inverness is a twenty-minute drive away and regular flights and trains provide easy access from any part of the country. Taxis are available to whisk you to Farley on arrival at either the airport or the station.
>
> *The moors and mountains stretching into the distance behind Farley*

Figure 3.12: Inserting a textbox

- To get rid of the line around the textbox, click it to select it and then click the arrow next to the **Line Color** tool on the Drawing toolbar. Select **No Line**.

Inserting WordArt

Underneath the picture we will insert a caption "*Ideal for walkers*".

- Position the insertion point beneath the picture and click the **Insert WordArt** button on the Drawing toolbar.

- Select a suitable style and type the text *Ideal for walkers*. Click **OK**. The text will be inserted in your chosen style and you can move and size it. Save the document.

Your brochure should now look something like Figure 3.13.

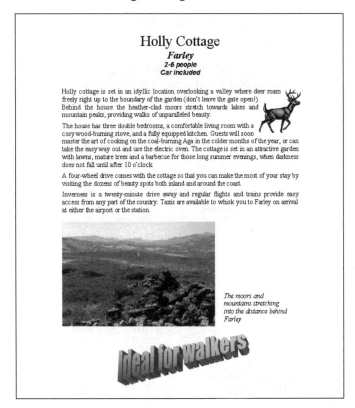

Figure 3.13: The holiday brochure

3.8 Inserting a table into a document

Next we will insert a table of prices into a new page in our holiday brochure.

- Starting on a new page, type the heading *Prices per week* and make it large, bold and centred.

You will insert a table and fill it in as shown in Figure 3.14.

- With the insertion point on a new line, click the **Insert Table** tool on the Standard toolbar.
- Drag across the grid to make a 4 x 2 table. A blank table is inserted into your document.
- Click in any cell of the table and select **Table**, **Table Properties**.
- Click the **Table** tab and select **Center** alignment. This centres the whole table.
- You can make the columns narrower by dragging a column border.
- Fill in the text as shown in Figure 3.14. You can centre the text in the second column by selecting the cells and then pressing the **Center** button on the Formatting toolbar.

Prices per week

	Low Season
Holly Cottage	£350
Oak Cottage	£375
Elm Cottage	£400

Figure 3.14: A table inserted into a document

To insert a column for **High Season** rates you can either select **Table**, **Insert** or you can split the cells in the second column. We'll try that.

- Drag over the cells in the second column to select them.
- Select **Table**, **Split Cells** and choose the settings shown below.

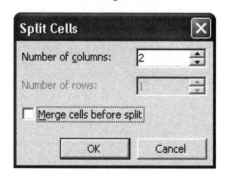

Figure 3.15: Splitting table cells

- Now enter a new heading and some High Season rates.

	Low Season	High Season
Holly Cottage	£350	£500
Oak Cottage	£375	£550
Elm Cottage	£400	£600

Figure 3.16

> **Note:** You can remove the borders, shade selected cells, etc using the **Borders and Shading** command on the **Format** menu. If you need more rows in a table, put the cursor in the last cell and press the **Tab** key. You can also select various options on the **Table** menu.

- That ends this task, so save and close your document.

The brochure is not finished, but you have learned the techniques to be able to create and complete something similar of your own.

> **Sample task: Create an advertising flyer using bullets, numbering, tabs, tables, borders and shading**

3.9   Margins and tabs

Setting margins

When you open a new document the page size, margins and tab stops will all have default values. You can change the default margins and page size as follows.

- Open a new document.

- From the menu select **File, Page Setup…** The following dialogue box is displayed (though your margins will probably be set differently).

- Change the margins to 3cm all round.

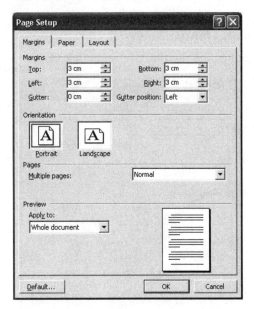

Figure 3.17: Setting the page margins

- You can alter the size and orientation of the page (e.g. from Portrait to Landscape) by clicking the **Paper** tab and selecting appropriate options. Leave the orientation as **Portrait**, and the paper size as **A4**.

Setting tab stops

The tabs in a new document will also be set to default values. As soon as you open a new or existing document, you will see the ruler line with default tabs. There are four different types of tab stops: left, right, centred and decimal. It is easiest to set tabs from the ruler line.

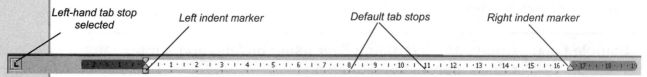

Figure 3.18: The ruler line

The default tabs on the ruler line shown in Figure 3.18 are all left-hand tabs one cm apart. If you were to set another tab stop, it would be another left tab, because the symbol for a left tab is showing at the left-hand end of the ruler line. (Measurements may be in either inches or centimetres – this can be changed using **Tools, Options,** clicking the **General** tab and making a selection in the **Measurement Units** box.)

- Type a heading: *Up to 50% off the price of a new car!!* Make it large, bold and centred.
- Type the text: *Fabulous savings can be made by buying your new right-hand drive car on the continent. For example:*

Now you are going to enter a tabulated list. First of all, change the default tab stops to 3cm as follows:

- From the menu select **Format, Tabs…**
- A dialogue box appears. Change the default tabs and click **OK**.

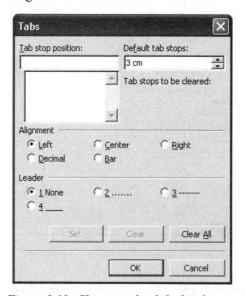

Figure 3.19: Changing the default tab stops

- Enter the items as shown below, separated by tabs. (Use the **Tab** key, located above the **Caps Lock** key on the keyboard, to move to the next tab stop.)

Make	UK Price	Europe
BMW 328i	£19,950	£14,500
Mazda 323	£11,770	£5,900
Porsche Boxter	£35,000	£28,000

- Select the whole list by dragging across it.

- Drag the left indent marker to the 3cm position. (See Figure 3.18.)

- Now select the table entries without the heading line.

- At the left-hand end of the ruler line, change the **Left tab** to **Right tab** by clicking it until the **Right tab** icon shows. (See Figure 3.20.)

- Insert two new tab stops at about 7.5 and 10.25. This right-aligns the currency amounts, as shown in Figure 3.20.

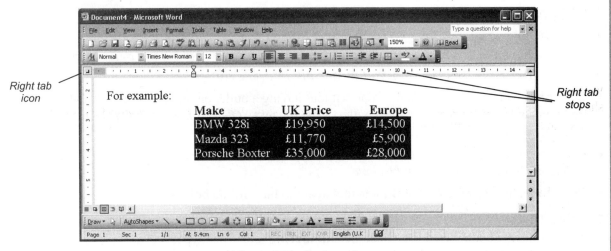

Figure 3.20: Setting tab stops

Adding a border and shading

- Select the whole table and click the **Outside Border** tool. The border will extend from the left margin to the right margin, and looks unbalanced.

- Drag the Right Indent marker on the ruler line to the left to about 10.75cm.

- Select the title line only, and from the menu select **Format, Borders and Shading**.

- In the dialogue box click the **Shading** tab, and choose a shading of about 15% as shown below. Click **OK**.

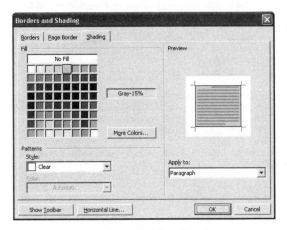

Figure 3.21: Adding Shading

- Don't forget to save your document regularly. Save it as **EuropCars.doc** in a suitable folder.

3.10 Bulleted and numbered lists

To create a bulleted list, you can either type the list first, and then select it before clicking the **Bullets** tool on the Formatting toolbar, or you can click the **Bullets** tool first and then type the list. We'll do that.

- Click underneath your price list to move the insertion point to a new line.
- Type: *The EuropCars Guide tells you how to make these incredible savings!*
- Press **Enter** to go to a new line.
- Click the **Bullets** tool on the Formatting toolbar.
- Type the following:
    - *We have researched the prices of thousands of new right-hand drive cars.*
    - *We list these prices for you in sterling in every edition.*
- Sometimes you want to go to a new line without having a bullet on the line. Press **Shift-Enter** to go to a new line that does not have a bullet. Type the text *YOU WILL BE ABLE TO COMPARE PRICES WITH THOSE OFFERED BY YOUR UK DEALER!*
- When you press **Enter**, the bullets start again. Type *We then list the dealers for you in France, Belgium, Holland, Germany and Ireland.*
- Press **Enter** twice and click the **Bullets** tool again to turn off the bullets.
- Type: *It's as easy as One-Two-Three!* and then press **Enter**.
- Now we'll type a numbered list. Click the **Numbering** tool. Then type:
    1. *Dial 09568 835 212 and press Start when you hear the Fax tone to print out a list of car prices and dealers.*
    2. *Call 0800 333777 and we will give you a voucher for 2 return tickets to Paris on EuroStar for only £10!*
    3. *Bring the car back and go through a simple process of registering it in the UK.*
- Press **Enter** and click the **Numbering** tool again to turn off the numbers.

Your page should look like Figure 3.22.

Up to 50% off the price of a new car!!

Fabulous savings can be made by buying your new right-hand drive car on the continent.

For example:

Make	UK Price	Europe
BMW 328i	£19,950	£14,500
Mazda 323	£11,770	£5,900
Porsche Boxter	£35,000	£28,000

The EuropCars guide tells you how to make these incredible savings!
- We have researched the prices of thousands of new right-hand drive cars.
- We list these prices for you in sterling in every edition.
  YOU WILL BE ABLE TO COMPARE PRICES WITH THOSE OFFERED BY YOUR UK DEALER!
- We then list the dealers for you in France, Belgium, Holland, Germany and Ireland.

It's as easy as One-Two-Three!
1. Dial 09568 835 212 and press Start when you hear the Fax tone to print out a list of car prices and dealers.
2. Call 0800 333777 and we will give you a voucher for 2 return tickets to Paris on EuroStar for only £10!
3. Bring the car back and go through a simple process of registering it in the UK.

Figure 3.22: Borders, shading, bullets and numbered lists

You can customise bulleted and numbered lists by selecting the list, then selecting **Format, Bullets and Numbering** from the menu. In the dialogue box, click the **Customize** button. The following dialogue box is displayed.

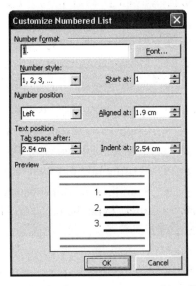

Figure 3.23: Customising a numbered list

You can alter the indents, the numbering style and the starting number.

- Save and close your advertisement.

3.11 Relating this chapter to the specification

Specification Reference (Part B)	What you have done to satisfy this
IT2.1	
Select information relevant to the tasks	• Using the Internet to find text and images • Searching the Internet using search engines • Finding holiday brochures • Choosing appropriate information and pictures for brochure and advertising flyers • Writing up your own experiences • Scanning in your own photographs
IT2.2	
Enter and combine information using formats that help development	• Formatting text • Using cut and paste/drag and drop • Importing images • Using tables • Bulleted and numbered lists • Tab stops • Trying out different images and formatting to suit the purpose
Develop information and derive new information as appropriate	• Developing the document format
IT2.3	
Develop the presentation so that the final output is accurate and shows consistent use of formats	• Text formatting • Paragraph formatting • Table formatting • Use of WordArt • Using Find and Replace for editing • Using spell-check and proof reading
Use layout appropriate to the types of information	• Margins • Consistent styles • Use of a text box for caption • Borders and shading • Tables

9.12   Other Key Skills signposting

Communication   C2.3 A document that includes at least one image.

9.13 Evidence for your portfolio

You may choose to produce several different word-processed documents as part of your evidence. You could, however develop these into larger tasks by integrating with other applications. An example of this would be to insert a spreadsheet into a word-processed document as described in Chapter 4. Examples of evidence that you could produce include:

♦ a word processed assignment for your main area of study (including a spreadsheet or chart if appropriate)

♦ a letter applying for a job together with a C.V.

♦ a price list for a hairdressing salon

♦ a report including tables and possibly a spreadsheet or a chart

♦ a restaurant menu

♦ an advertising leaflet

Type of evidence	✔
A brief written description of the activity	
A hand-drawn sketch of each document's rough layout	
Notes of the sources of information and images	
Working drafts of the documents showing corrections needed and why	
Screenshots to show spell-check/find and replace in action	
Screenshots from Explorer to show the saved file	
Final printouts of the documents	
Record from your assessor of how you developed the content and presentation of your work	

9.14 Sample questions

Questions 1-6 refer to the advertisement shown on the right:

NEW!! NEW!! NEW!!
Opening Soon –
the *hottest* spot in town

Raffertys Night Club

12, Kingston Street, Ipswich

● Great Music
● Cheap drinks
● Fantastic atmosphere

Open 8 'til late ●●●
Thursday   Happy hour 8-9pm
Friday   DJ Steve Coolins
Saturday   Your kind of music

1. The text in the shaded area is
   A   aligned left
   B   centered
   C   fully justified
   D   aligned right

2. The address of the nightclub is formatted
   A   bold
   B   italic
   C   underlined
   D   aligned right

3. The information underneath the address is formatted as a
   A   numbered list
   B   bulleted list
   C   table
   D   chart

4. The text at the bottom of the advert will probably have been inserted using a
   A   text box
   B   3D effect
   C   circle tool
   D   WordArt design

5. The image is Clip Art taken from the Internet. Which of these are NOT techniques for formatting images?
   A   cropping
   B   sizing
   C   text wrapping
   D   analogising

6. The black circles in the bottom section were created using the oval tool. Which of these techniques cannot be applied to shapes drawn in this way?
   A   fill with colour
   B   change line colour
   C   rotate
   D   split cells

Chapter 4 – Introduction to Spreadsheets

Objectives

- ❑ To enter text labels, numbers and formulae into a spreadsheet
- ❑ To change column widths, row heights, insert and delete rows and columns as required
- ❑ To refine the layout by formatting text and numbers, adding borders and shading
- ❑ To explore the effects of changing information in a spreadsheet model
- ❑ To generate charts and graphs from spreadsheet data
- ❑ To link a spreadsheet and chart to a word-processed document so that when figures are changed, the changes are reflected in the word-processed document

---

Sample task: Set up a planning budget for a ski holiday

In this task you must imagine that you are in charge of planning a ski holiday with a group of friends. You have chosen your destination, and now have to choose method of travel, accommodation, ski lift passes/lessons etc. to fit within each person's budget by setting up a Microsoft Excel spreadsheet model.

4.1   Finding the information for this type of activity

Clearly before you begin to set up this type of spreadsheet model you would need to find out some facts and figures. You may use your own past experiences, look back at invoices or bills you have paid for this type of holiday and use that information. Or you could look up the information in winter holiday brochures from the travel agents. Another option is the many Internet sites that offer this type of holiday – detailed prices are often given that you could use in your spreadsheet model.

Record the sources of your information on an Information Seeking record sheet (a sample is provided at www.payne-gallway.co.uk/ksit).

For this sample activity you are given the information to use in the spreadsheet.

4.2   Introducing Excel 2003

Excel 2003 is one of a number of powerful spreadsheet packages. Excel files are known as **workbooks,** with each workbook consisting of one or more worksheets. A **worksheet** is like a page from an accountant's ledger, divided into rows and columns which you can fill with text, numbers and formulae.

(The term **spreadsheet** is used rather loosely nowadays to mean either a worksheet or a workbook.)

Microsoft Office Excel 2003

- Start Excel by double-clicking the Excel icon on the desktop or selecting **Start, Programs, Microsoft Excel**.

Excel will open a new workbook. By default the workbook has 3 worksheets, and the Sheet tab at the bottom of the workbook shows that **Sheet1** is currently displayed.

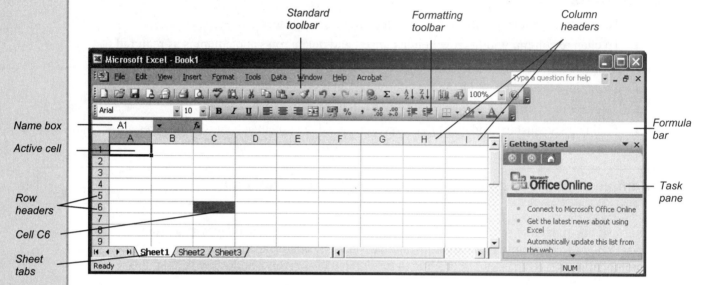

Figure 4.1: An Excel workbook

4.3   Moving round the worksheet

When you open a new workbook, **Sheet1** is displayed with cell **A1** highlighted. Cells are named according to the row and column they are in; cell C6 is thus at the intersection of Column C, Row 6. The cell with the heavy border around it is the **active cell** (A1 in Figure 4.1). If you start typing, anything you type will appear in the active cell, and also in the Formula bar.

You can move around the worksheet to make a cell active in any of these ways:

- Use the mouse to click in the cell you want.
- Use one of the arrow keys to go up, down, left or right.
- Use the **Page Up** or **Page Down** keys.
- Press **Ctrl-G** or select **Edit, Go To** from the menu and type in the cell reference to go to. Try going to cell **AH2000**.
- Press **Ctrl-Home** to return to A1.

As you can see, the spreadsheet is much larger than the portion of it that you can see on the screen. You can also use the scroll bars to move around the spreadsheet.

- Press **Ctrl-Right Arrow**, and then **Ctrl-Down Arrow** to get to the last cell in the spreadsheet. What is its cell reference?

The Task pane opens and closes automatically depending on what you are doing. You can close the Task pane at any time by clicking the **Close** icon in its top right-hand corner. You can reopen the Task pane from the **View** menu.

- Close the Task pane.

4.4   Entering and copying text, numbers and formulae

To start with, you will create a spreadsheet set out like Figure 4.2.

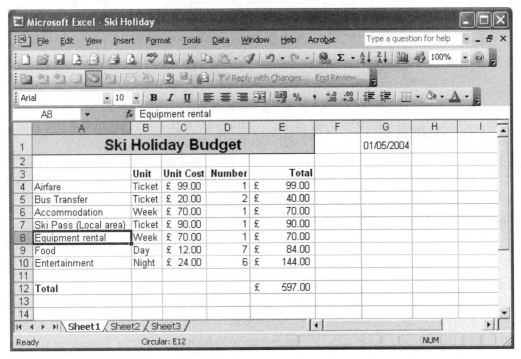

Figure 4.2: A budget spreadsheet

- With the cursor in cell A1, type the heading *Ski Holiday Budget*. Press **Enter**.

- Double-click between the column headers A and B to autosize column A so that the heading fits in cell A1.

- Use the mouse or the arrow keys to move to cell B3.

- Enter the other text and numbers as shown in Figure 4.3. Notice that text labels are automatically left-justified, while numbers are automatically right-justified.

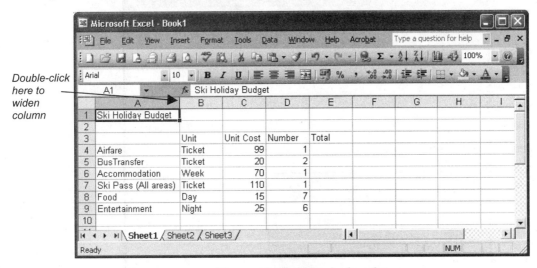

Figure 4.3: Entering budget data

Entering formulae

The real power of a spreadsheet lies in its ability to calculate the results of formulae which reference other cells in the workbook. The following mathematical symbols are used:

+	(add)
-	(subtract)
*	(multiply)
/	(divide)
()	(brackets)

- In cell E4, enter the formula *=C4*D4* and press **Enter**. (You can use either uppercase or lowercase letters, but you must start the formula with the = sign to tell Excel that this is a formula and not a label.) The answer, 99, appears in the cell.

- Try another way of entering a formula. In cell E5, type =, and then click in cell C5. Type * and then click in cell D5. Press **Enter**. This technique is called *entering a formula by pointing*. It has the great advantage that you are less likely to enter the wrong cell reference by mistake.

Copying and pasting cells

There are several ways to copy and paste cell contents in Excel. One of the quickest and easiest is to use the **Fill handle**.

- Click in cell E5.

- Drag the small handle in the bottom right-hand corner down to cell E9. The formula is copied to cells E6 to E9, adjusting automatically to reference cells in the correct row.

- Click in cell E9 and take a look at the Formula bar, which shows that the formula in that cell is C9*D9.

Try a different way of copying cells. We will copy the budget to cells starting in A12.

- Drag across from cell A1 to E9 to select all these cells. Click the **Copy** button, select **Edit, Copy** from the menu, or right-click and select **Copy**. A moving dotted border appears around the selected cells.

- Right-click in cell A12 and select **Paste**. All the cells are copied.

Now your spreadsheet should look like this:

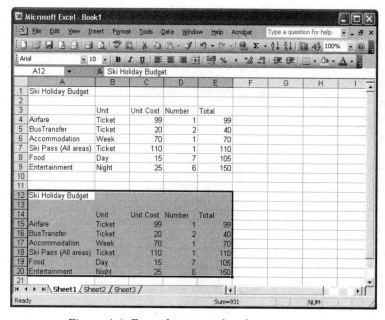

Figure 4.4: Formulae entered and range copied

4.5   Saving a workbook

You should save your workbook before you do any more work on it.

- Click the **Save** icon or select **File, Save** from the menu.

- By default the workbook will be named **Book1** and saved in the **My Documents** folder.

- You need to have an appropriate folder in which to store all your **Key Skills in IT** work (see Chapter 2). If you have not got one, you can click the button as shown in Figure 4.5 to create one. Alternatively, you may be saving your work on a floppy disk, in which case you should select **A:** instead of **My Documents** in the list box.

- Name the workbook *Ski Holiday*. Excel gives it the extension *.xls*.

- Click **Save**.

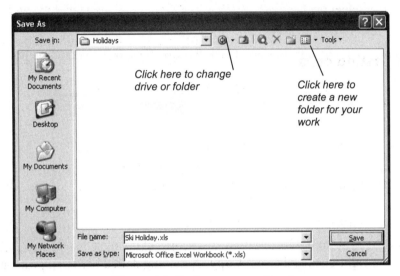

Figure 4.5: Saving your workbook

4.6   Formatting the worksheet

You should have the workbook **Ski Holiday.xls** open to continue with this exercise.

Adjusting column widths

You have already seen that by double-clicking the right-hand border of a column header, the column width is adjusted so that the text or numbers in the column fit without overflowing into the next column. You can adjust several column widths at once.

- Drag across the column headers A to E to select all those columns.

- Double-click the border between any two of the column headers. All the column widths will be adjusted so that the text exactly fits.

- You can widen any of the columns by dragging the border between its column header and the next column header to the right. Widen column E to about 12.00 – a Tip appears when you position the cursor to drag the border to tell you how wide the column is.

Formatting text

First we will centre the heading Ski Holiday Budget, increase its font size and make it bold.

- Drag across cells A1 to E1 to select the range.

- Click the **Merge and Center** button on the Formatting toolbar. This merges the 5 cells into a single cell with the cell reference A1.

- With cell A1 still selected, change the font size to **16** by clicking the **Font Size** button.
- Make the heading bold by clicking the **Bold** button.
- Click Row Header 3 to select the whole row.
- Click the **Bold** button to make all the headings bold.
- The heading **Total** needs to be right-aligned so that it is over the numbers. The headings **Unit Cost** and **Number** could be right-aligned too, in case we later decide to make columns C and D wider. Select these three headings and press the **Align Right** button on the Formatting toolbar.

Adding borders and shading

You can add a border to a single cell or a group of cells. We will add a border and shading to cell A1.

- Click in cell A1 to select the heading.
- From the menu select **Format, Cells…**
- The **Format cells** dialogue box appears. Click the **Border** tab. The dialogue box appears as shown in Figure 4.6.

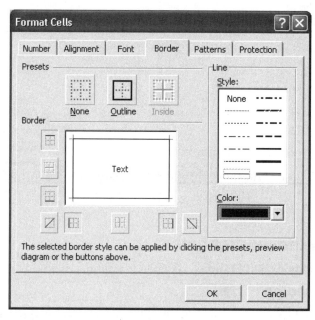

Figure 4.6: Inserting a border

- Select a line style, choose a colour and click the **Outline** button. Click **OK**. (You must choose the line style and set the colour *before* clicking the **Outline** button.)
- Click the **Fill Color** button on the Formatting toolbar and choose a suitable colour.

Formatting numbers

Columns C and E both need to be formatted to 2 decimal places, since they contain currency amounts. You may also decide to put a £ sign in front of each number.

- Select column C by clicking its column header.
- You can now select column E by keeping the **Ctrl** key pressed while you click column header E.
- From the menu select **Format, Cells**.
- In the dialogue box click the **Number** tab, and select **Currency** in the list box as shown in Figure 4.7.

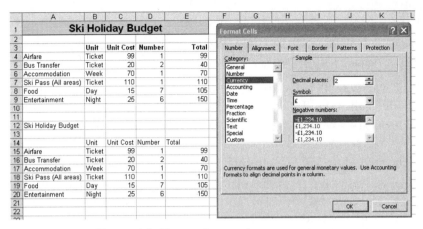

	A	B	C	D	E							
1	**Ski Holiday Budget**											
2												
3		Unit	Unit Cost	Number	Total							
4	Airfare	Ticket	99	1	99							
5	Bus Transfer	Ticket	20	2	40							
6	Accommodation	Week	70	1	70							
7	Ski Pass (All areas)	Ticket	110	1	110							
8	Food	Day	15	7	105							
9	Entertainment	Night	25	6	150							
10												
11												
12	Ski Holiday Budget											
13												
14		Unit	Unit Cost	Number	Total							
15	Airfare	Ticket	99	1	99							
16	Bus Transfer	Ticket	20	2	40							
17	Accommodation	Week	70	1	70							
18	Ski Pass (All areas)	Ticket	110	1	110							
19	Food	Day	15	7	105							
20	Entertainment	Night	25	6	150							
21												
22												

Figure 4.7: Formatting numbers as currency

- Click **OK**.

An alternative way of formatting cells as Currency is to select the cells and then click the **Currency** button on the toolbar.

- Select E4 to E9 and click the **Currency** button. The formatting is slightly different. Decide which format you prefer and make columns C and E the same format.

Entering and formatting dates

- In cell G1, enter the date *01/05/04* and press **Enter**.

Excel recognises this as a date, and you can format it in a selection of different ways. Instead of using the menu command **Format, Cells…**, you can use the shortcut menu this time.

- Right-click cell G1 and select **Format Cells…**

- In the dialogue box click the **Number** tab, and select **Date**. Select a format such as **14/03/01**. If the date appears as 03/14/01 your system is set up to display dates in American format. To change this, do the following:

- Select **Start, Control Panel**.

- Double-click **Regional and Language Options**. Make sure the **Regional Options** tab is selected and that **English (United Kingdom)** is selected.

- Note that the Short date format is **dd/MM/yyyy**.

- Click **OK**. You will have to restart your computer before any new settings take effect, so be sure to save your work before you restart.

4.7   Inserting and deleting rows and columns

The organiser of this ski holiday has forgotten to enter the cost of ski (or snowboard) and boot rental.

- Right-click row header 8. Select **Insert**. A new row is inserted.

- Type the text *Equipment rental*, *Week*, *£70*, *1*.

- Practise deleting several rows at a time. Drag across row headers 17 to 21, right-click, and select **Delete**.

- Drag across row headers 13 to 16 and delete the rest of the bottom spreadsheet.

You can insert columns in the same way. Alternatively, you can select **Rows** or **Columns** from the **Insert** menu.

- Remember to save your work frequently.

4.8 What if?

Now we need to calculate the total of all expenses and make sure it is within everyone's budget.

- In A12, type *Total*. Make it bold.

- Make cell E12 the active cell, and click the **AutoSum** button on the Standard toolbar. A dotted line appears around cells E4 to E11, showing that these are the cells which will be summed. It is a good idea to include the extra blank row in case you later decide to add an extra row to the list of expenses.

- Press **Enter**. The total of the column appears, £644.

Now supposing that you have told everyone that the holiday will cost no more than £600. You will have to find some way of reducing the costs. There are various options; a cheaper ski pass which does not cover all areas in the region could be purchased for £90, you could spend less on food, select cheaper accommodation etc.

Let's try out the effect of spending only £12 per day on food.

- In cell C9, type *12*. The total cost reduces to £623.

- In cell C7, type *90*. Double-click in cell A7 and change the text to *Ski Pass (local area)*. Widen the column.

- In cell C10, type *24* for **Entertainment**. There! The total is now £597.00.

Of course, you have not budgeted for emergencies, and some people may want the full lift pass. So you can keep trying out different options until you have the best deal possible.

4.9 Printing the spreadsheet

It is essential to have a look at what your document will look like when printed before actually printing it. You need to make sure that the correct range of cells will be printed, that it fits neatly onto the page, and that you have selected the correct orientation (Portrait or Landscape).

- Click the **Print Preview** button on the Standard toolbar.

- A preview of the page appears. You can click the **Zoom** button to get a larger view of the page.

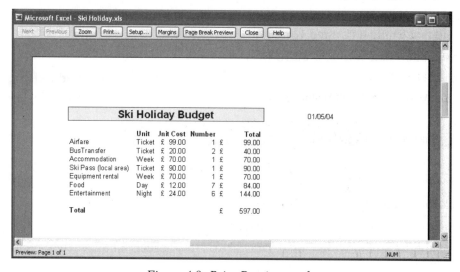

Figure 4.8: Print Preview mode

There are buttons along the top of the screen in Print Preview mode.

- Click the **Setup...** button.

The Page Setup dialogue box appears, and you can change from Portrait to Landscape, make a large spreadsheet fit on a single page, etc.

Note that you can also display this dialogue box by selecting **File, Page Setup** from the menu bar when you are in Normal view with the spreadsheet on screen.

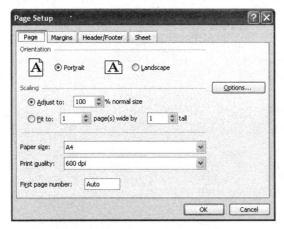

Figure 4.9: The Page Setup dialogue box

- You can print the spreadsheet by clicking the **Print** button.

- Experiment with the **Margins** and **Page Break Preview** buttons. You can always get back to Normal view by selecting **View, Normal** from the menu.

- To return to Normal view from Print Preview, click the **Close** button or press **Escape.**

4.10 Inserting a spreadsheet into a word-processed document

You may want to include the spreadsheet in a letter to one or more group members. First, you must copy the spreadsheet to the Clipboard.

- Select cells A1 to E12 and select **Edit, Copy** from the menu.

- Open Word, and type the text

  Dear Bob
  Here's the ski holiday budget.

- Press **Enter** twice.

- From the menu select **Edit, Paste Special**. A dialogue box appears as shown in Figure 4.10.

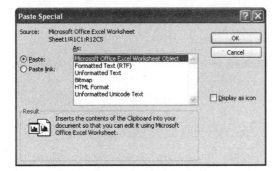

Figure 4.10: Pasting a spreadsheet

- Make sure that **Paste** and **Microsoft Excel Worksheet** are selected, and click **OK**.

- The spreadsheet will be inserted into your document. You can move it by dragging it.

- Save the document in a suitable folder, calling it **Letter to Bob**.
- Type *Hope this looks OK* underneath the spreadsheet. The letter should look like Figure 4.11.

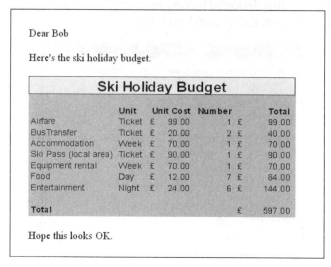

Figure 4.11: Word document with spreadsheet inserted

Note that the highlighting is copied over, but will not print out. You can edit the spreadsheet right in the Word document. The changes will not be reflected in the original spreadsheet though, because the spreadsheet in the Word document is not linked to the original, but simply embedded in the letter.

- Double-click the spreadsheet in the Word document. It opens in Excel and you can edit it as required.

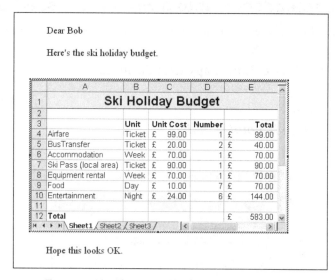

Figure 4.12: The spreadsheet ready to be edited

- Change cell C9 to *£10*. The total changes to £583.00.
- Click away from the spreadsheet.
- Save and close the Word document.
- Save and close the **Ski Holiday** spreadsheet.

> **Sample task:** **Create a spreadsheet and chart of monthly average maximum and minimum temperatures to insert in a holiday brochure**

In this task we will create a chart of temperatures which could be inserted, for example, into the holiday brochure created in Chapter 3.

First of all the figures need to be entered into a new spreadsheet.

- Click the **New** icon on the standard toolbar.
- In cell A1 type the heading *Average Daily Temperatures*.
- In cell B3, type *Maximum*. In cell C3, type *Minimum*.
- In cell A4 type *January*.

Copying series

Excel has a clever feature which enables you to fill in the other months of the year very quickly.

- Drag the corner handle of cell A4 down to cell A15 and release it. The other eleven months of the year are automatically filled in.
- Fill in the figures as shown in Figure 4.13.
- Format the labels as shown, widening columns where necessary.
- Save your spreadsheet in a suitable folder, calling it **Temperatures**.

	A	B	C	D
1	Average Daily Temperatures			
2				
3		Maximum	Minimum	
4	January	5	1	
5	February	8	2	
6	March	10	3	
7	April	12	5	
8	May	14	8	
9	June	18	10	
10	July	22	13	
11	August	24	15	
12	September	19	13	
13	October	16	10	
14	November	11	5	
15	December	8	2	
16				
17	Average			
18				

Figure 4.13: The figures to be entered in the spreadsheet

4.11 Using functions

You have already used one function – the **Sum** function. This is so often required that it has its own button on the toolbar. However, Excel has hundreds of other useful functions which work with numbers and text. We will try out four of these functions.

We will use functions to find the average maximum and minimum monthly temperatures, the highest and lowest figures in each column, and a count of the number of temperatures we have entered (Yes, I know it's 12, but with a large spreadsheet this is often a useful function!)

- In cell A17 type *Average* as shown in Figure 4.13.
- Make cell B17 the active cell by clicking in it or moving to it, and click the **Insert Function** button on the Standard toolbar.

- A dialogue box appears. In the Category list select **Statistical** and then select the **Average** function as shown in Figure 4.14.

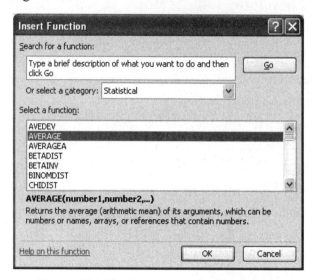

Figure 4.14: The Paste Function dialogue box

- Click **OK**. A further dialogue box appears, which you can move out of the way of the figures by dragging.

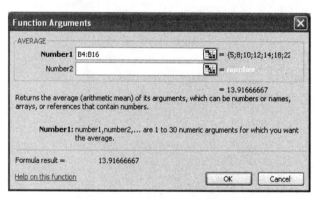

Figure 4.15: Entering the range of cells to average

Excel correctly guesses the range of cells to average. However, we are never going to have a 13th month so you can edit the range.

- In the **Number1** box, edit the range so that it is **B4:B15**.
- Click **OK**. The average maximum temperature for the year is entered.

- Format the average by clicking the **Decrease Decimal** button on the Formatting toolbar until the number is displayed to only one decimal place.
- Type the labels *Highest* and *Lowest* in cells A18 and A19.
- In cell B18, use the function **Max** to find the Maximum value in the column.
- In cell B19, use the function **Min** to find the Minimum value in the column.
- In cell A20 type the label *Number of Months*. Widen the column.
- In cell B20, use the function **Count** to count the number of months from Row 4 to Row 15.
- Copy the formulae to column C by selecting cells B17 to B20, and dragging the corner handle to the next column.

The results should appear as in Figure 4.16.

	A	B	C	D
1	Average Daily Temperatures			
2				
3		Maximum	Minimum	
4	January	5	1	
5	February	8	2	
6	March	10	3	
7	April	12	5	
8	May	14	8	
9	June	18	10	
10	July	22	13	
11	August	24	15	
12	September	19	13	
13	October	16	10	
14	November	11	5	
15	December	8	2	
16				
17	Average	13.9	7.3	
18	Highest	24	15	
19	Lowest	5	1	
20	Number of Months	12	12	
21				

Figure 4.16: Using functions

4.12 Creating a chart

Next we will create a bar chart showing the monthly maximum and minimum temperatures.

- Select the range A3 to C15.
- Click the **Chart Wizard** button on the Standard toolbar.

The Chart Wizard dialogue box appears as shown in Figure 4.17.

- Select **Column** as the Chart type.
- Press and hold the button to view the chart. Try changing the chart type to **Line**, and pressing the button again to see what the line graph would look like.
- Change back to **Column**, and click **Next**.

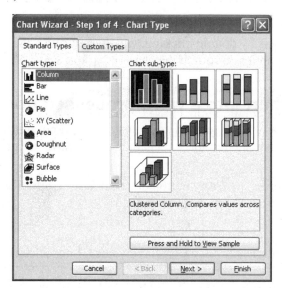

Figure 4.17: The Chart Wizard dialogue box

- Check that the correct range (A3:C15) is selected, and click **Next** in the Step 2 dialogue box.
- Fill in the Step 3 dialogue box as shown in Figure 4.18, and click **Next**.

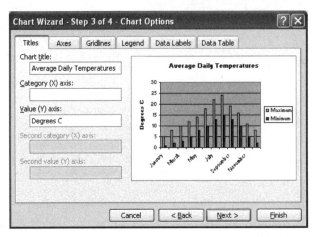

Figure 4.18: Entering chart title and axis labels

- Leave the option **As object in Sheet 1** selected, and click **Finish**.
- The chart appears in the worksheet. You can drag it out of the way of the figures.

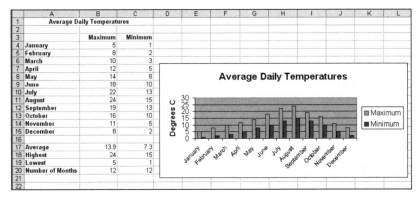

Figure 4.19: The chart inserted into the worksheet

You can make the chart bigger or smaller by dragging its corner handles. You can also change the font size of headings and labels by double-clicking, which brings up a dialogue box. Right-clicking one of the bars gives you an option to format the chart in various ways. Experiment!

4.13 Importing a chart into a word-processed document

You can import a chart into a word-processed document. We will put it into the holiday brochure *Holly Cottage.doc* which you created in the last chapter. If you have not got this, just open a new document instead.

- With the chart selected, press the **Copy** button or select **Edit, Copy** from the menu.
- Start Microsoft Word.
- Open **Holly Cottage.doc**.
- Go to the second page underneath Price List and on a new line, select **Edit, Paste Special.** The following dialogue box is selected.

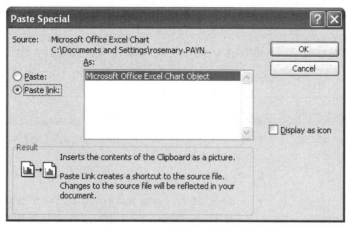

Figure 4.20

When you pasted a spreadsheet into the word-processed document **Ski Holiday** in the previous task, you selected **Paste** rather than **Paste Link** to paste it in. This meant that any changes you made to the spreadsheet in Excel would not be reflected in the Word document.

This time, you are going to try the other alternative, **Paste link**. Read the dialogue box for the explanation of what this means.

- Click **Paste Link** to select it and click **OK**. The chart will be inserted into the word-processed document.

- Now return to Excel, and change the Maximum temperature in July to 3. (A climatic catastrophe.)

- Go back to the Word document. The chart has automatically changed, because it is linked.

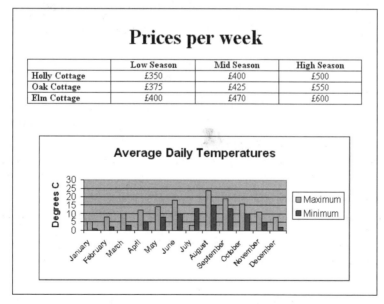

Figure 4.21: A chart in a Word document linked to the chart in Excel

- In Excel, undo your latest change.
- Save and close the spreadsheet **Temperatures.xls**.
- Save and close **Holly Cottages.doc** in Word.

4.14 Relating this chapter to the specification

Specification Reference (Part B)	What you have done to satisfy this
IT2.1	
Select information relevant to the tasks	• Find information on holiday expenses – from brochures, the Internet or personal experience. • Searching for appropriate web sites • Choosing relevant information to include in calculations.
IT2.2	
Enter and combine information using formats that help development	• Copy and paste • Formatting the worksheet
Develop information and derive new information as appropriate	• What if? calculations • Using formulae and functions • Producing charts • Inserting spreadsheet and charts into word processing
IT2.3	
Develop the presentation so that the final output is accurate and shows consistent use of formats	• Layout and formatting of spreadsheet • Layout and formatting of spreadsheet and chart in word processing document
Use layout appropriate to the types of information	• Refining the layout • Linking information • Creating a new folder and saving the documents • Proof reading

4.15 Other Key Skills signposting

Application of Number   N2.1 Interpret information

N2.2 Carry out calculations using formulae

N2.3 Interpret results of your calculations using a chart

4.16 Evidence for your portfolio

A spreadsheet can provide useful evidence for your portfolio. You need to find an application that interests you or that will be useful for one of your other subjects – or preferably both! Some possible ideas for using spreadsheets are given below:

◆ Logging results from a Science experiment, performing analyses, and including the spreadsheet and/or charts in a word-processed report

◆ Budgeting for an event such as a school trip, holiday etc.

◆ Recording daily or weekly sales of say a Farm shop, a school shop, or a hamburger stand.

◆ Keeping track of the stock of a small shop or sales outlet.

◆ Calculating expenses such as mileage, accommodation, meals etc for a business user.

◆ Looking up on the Internet and comparing prices for goods or services such as computers, flights etc. Recording these on a spreadsheet.

For any of these activities, the table below shows the evidence that you should include in your portfolio.

Type of evidence	✔
A brief written description of the activity	
Notes on the sources of information	
Working drafts of the documents showing corrections needed and why	
Printouts displaying the formulae used (see Chapter 8, section 8.12)	
Screenshots from Explorer to show the saved file	
Final printouts of the documents	
Record from your assessor of how you developed the content and presentation of your work	

4.17 Sample questions

Questions 1-6 relate to the following spreadsheet information:

A shop kept the following information about clothes they sold in one week. The selling price is what the customers paid for the items. The cost price is how much the shop paid the supplier for the items.

	A	B	C	D	E	F
1	Item of clothing	Selling Price	No. Sold	Gross sales value	Cost price	Net Profit
2	T. Shirts	£ 9.99	3	£ 29.97	£ 6.00	£ 23.97
3	Track suits	£ 35.99	14	£ 503.86	£ 28.00	£ 475.86
4	Dresses	£ 29.50	10	£ 295.00	£ 50.00	£ 245.00
5	Men's Suits	£ 99.99	1	£ 99.99	£ 20.00	£ 79.99
6	Ladies' suits	£ 75.50	2	£ 151.00	£ 30.00	£ 121.00
7	Trousers	£ 28.00	10	£ 280.00	£ 20.00	£ 260.00
8	Skirts	£ 25.00	28	£ 700.00	£ 56.00	£ 644.00
9					Grand Total	£1,849.82

1. If the shop sold an extra 2 skirts which cell would you have to change?

    A   C8

    B   B8

    C   A8

    D   C7

2. To calculate the total in cell F9 you would sum the cells

    A   E2 to E8

    B   F2 to F8

    C   A8 to F8

    D   E2 to F8

3. To calculate the net profit, you must subtract the Cost price from the Gross sales value. The formula in F2, therefore, is:

    A   D2-D3

    B   D2-E2

    C   C2-D2

    D   D3-D4

4. Which 2 cells would change if the entry in E8 was changed to £60?

    A   D8 and F8

    B   D8 and F9

    C   C8 and D8

    D   F8 and F9

5. If you wanted to remove skirts from the selling range, you would have to:

    A   Delete a column

    B   Delete a cell

    C   Delete some headings

    D   Delete a row

6. The formula in D6 is:

    A   B6*C6

    B   E6*C6

    C   C5*C6

    D   E6*F6

Chapter 5 – Introduction to Databases

Objectives

- ❑ To decide on the fields and data types that need to be stored in a database for a particular purpose
- ❑ To design and create a database structure
- ❑ To insert, edit and delete fields and records
- ❑ To sort data on one or more fields
- ❑ To use queries involving multiple criteria to search a database
- ❑ To create and format a report using data from the database
- ❑ To compare different report formats created using wizards and select the most suitable one for a given purpose

> **Sample task: Create and use a database of holiday cottage bookings**

In this chapter you will learn how to use Microsoft Access 2003 to create a database for a company that rents out cottages to holidaymakers during the summer months.

5.1   Finding the information and planning a database

Before you can start to design a database, there are several questions that need to be answered first. You need to establish:

- ♦ What is the purpose of the database?
- ♦ What information will the user need to extract from the database?
- ♦ What data will be put into the database?
- ♦ What format is the data in – numeric, text, dates, currency, Yes/No, or something else?
- ♦ What processing needs to be carried out on the data – do totals of some fields need to be calculated, for example?

You will need to discuss the requirements for the database with the user. Then you must find the information to enter into the database which might, for example, currently be held as paper records. These records may hold slightly different information from that to be stored in the Access database, so you will have to search for and select the appropriate information.

Remember to make a note of your sources of information and record them on an Information Seeking record sheet (a sample is provided at www.payne-gallway.co.uk/ksit).

For this sample activity suppose that you have interviewed the owner of the holiday cottages and have established the following facts.

1. The company owns 3 cottages named Holly, Elm and Oak.
2. The cottages are always rented by the week, starting on a Saturday.
3. Each cottage can sleep up to 6 people.
4. There is an optional extra charge for the daily services of a cleaner.
5. Each customer upon booking makes a deposit, which normally varies between £100 and £300.
6. The owner of the company wants the database to include the name and address of the customer making the booking so that he can write to them confirming the start and end date of the holiday and the amount of deposit already paid. He also wants the customer's telephone number to be recorded.
7. He wants to be able to query the database to find, for example, all bookings for a particular cottage between two specific dates.
8. He also wants to be able to produce a report which shows the bookings for each cottage for a given period, and the total amount of the deposits paid during that period.

5.2   Understanding field types

Once you have established what the input, processing and output requirements are, you can start designing the database structure. In this chapter we will be designing a database that involves only a single table. A more complex database would involve several tables linked together by common fields.

The first thing to do is to make a list of all the fields that will be required, and decide what field type to give to each one. Field types in an Access database include the following:

Data Type	Usage	Comments
Text	Alphanumeric data, i.e. any letter, number or other symbol that you can see on the keyboard	A field can be up to 255 characters
Number	Numeric data	Can choose a whole number or a number with a decimal point. Each of these categories has several choices in Access depending on the size of the numbers you want to store – e.g. a whole number can be defined as Byte (0-255), Integer (-32,768 to 32,767) or Long Integer (for larger numbers).
Date/Time	Dates and times	You should always use a Date/Time field for a date, not a text field, because Access can calculate with dates (e.g. find how many days between 03/09/2004 and 25/12/2004) but not with text.
Currency	For all monetary data	
Yes/No	True/False data	Useful when a field can only take one of two possible values such as Yes or No, True or False.
AutoNumber	Often used for a key field – i.e. one that uniquely identifies a record. No two records ever have the same key field.	This is a unique value generated by Access for each record.

Selecting fields

Each field in a record will hold one piece of information. But what is a piece of information? Is *Name* one piece of information, or should it be broken down into *Title* (Mr, Ms etc) *First name* and *Surname*?

There are several reasons for splitting *Name* into 3 fields.

1. If you want to sort the customers' records alphabetically by surname, you will not be able to do so unless *Surname* is a separate field.

2. You may want to search for a particular customer record. It is much easier to search on Surname.

3. The names and addresses will be used in a mail merge, which involves putting fields from the database in a standard letter. You will want to be able to start the letter, for example, 'Dear Mr Harris', not 'Dear Mr L. Harris'. Therefore, you must hold the surname, title and initial in separate fields. Similarly, you will need each line of the address in separate fields so that you can put the address at the top of the letter and possibly on the envelope as well, on separate lines.

Deciding on data types

You will have to decide on the data type for each field. For example, should you hold *Telephone Number* as a Text field or a Number field? At first you may think that a Number field would be best but in practice this is a bad idea for two reasons:

1. Access will not record leading zeroes in a number field. So if the telephone number is 0149450 it will be recorded as 149450 which is incorrect.

2. Access will not allow you to put a space, bracket or hyphen in a number field. So you will not be able to record a telephone number as, for example, 01473 874512.

5.3   Designing the database structure

The next stage is to decide on field names for each field and write down a list of the fields that you are going to need in your database. The fields will be stored in a **table**, and you will have to choose a name for the table as well. One common convention is to use a table name beginning with **tbl**. We will call our table **tblBooking**.

Another sensible convention is not to have any spaces in your field names. That way you don't have to try and remember whether or not the name has a space in it. Uppercase letters can be used in the middle of a field name to make it easy to read.

Each record in the database should be given a unique key field. In this table, it could be **BookingNumber** and have type **AutoNumber**.

tblBooking

Field name	Data Type
BookingNumber	AutoNumber
Title	Text
Initial	Text
Surname	Text
Address1	Text
Address2	Text
Postcode	Text
Telephone	Text
StartDate	Date/Time
EndDate	Date/Time
Cottage	Text
Deposit	Currency
CleaningService	Yes/No
NumberInParty	Number (Integer)

*Figure 5.1: Structure of **tblBooking***

5.4 Creating a new database

Loading Access

The way that you load Access will depend on which version of Access you are using and whether you are working at home or on a school or college network. There may be an icon in the Main Window or Applications Window that you can click on, or you can click the Access icon in the Office Shortcut Bar at the top of the screen if this is visible. In Windows 95 and later versions you can click on **Start** in the bottom left-hand corner and select **Programs, Microsoft Access**.

Creating a new database

When you first start Access, you have the option of either opening an existing database or creating a new one. Access provides many ready-made databases for you to use, and also several wizards to help you to quickly create a database. However in this case, we will create a new database from scratch.

You will see a screen similar to the one shown below.

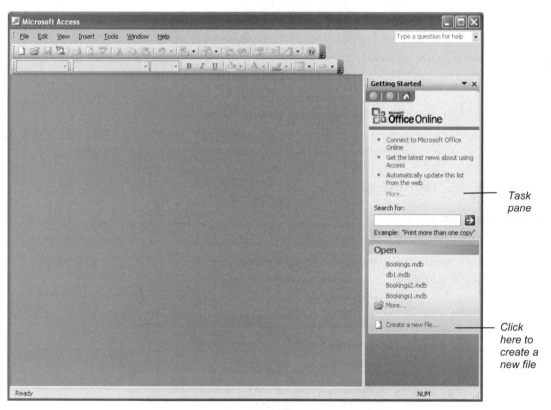

Figure 5.2: Starting MS Access

- Click on **Create a new file** in the Task pane. On the next screen click **Blank database**.

A window opens as shown in Figure 5.3, asking you to select a folder and a name for your new database. It is a good idea to keep each Access database in its own folder.

- Click the **Create New Folder** button and create a new folder named **Holidays**.

- In the **File Name** box, type the name *Cottages.mdb* and press the **Create** button.

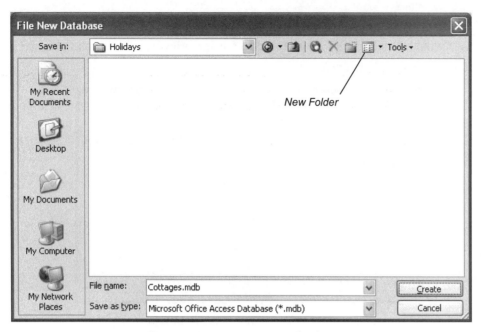

Figure 5.3: Naming a new database

5.5   Creating a new table

All data in an Access database is stored in **tables**. A table has a row for each record, and a column for each field. The first thing you have to do is to tell Access exactly what fields you want in each record, and what data type each field is. This is referred to as the database table **structure**. After this has been done and the structure saved, you can start adding data to the database.

The Database window

Every Access database has a database window. The window has buttons for each type of database object: **Tables, Queries, Forms, Reports,** etc. In addition, there are options to open an object, change its design, or create a new object. **Tables** is currently selected and since at the moment there are no existing tables to Open or Design, only the Create options are active.

Figure 5.4: The Database window

Creating a new table

In the Database window make sure **Create table in Design View** is selected and click **New**. A new window appears as shown below.

Figure 5.5: Creating a new table in Design view

- Select **Design View** and click **OK**. The Table Design window appears.

- Look back at the design for **tblBooking** in Figure 5.1. All these fields need to be entered in the new table.

- Enter the first field name, **BookingNumber**, and tab to the Data Type column.

- Click the Down arrow and select the field type **AutoNumber**.

- Tab to the Description column and type *This is the Key field*. Notice that in the Field Properties list below, **AutoNumber** is automatically given a Field Size property of **Long Integer**. New Values has the property **Increment**, which means that this field will automatically be increased by 1 for each new customer.

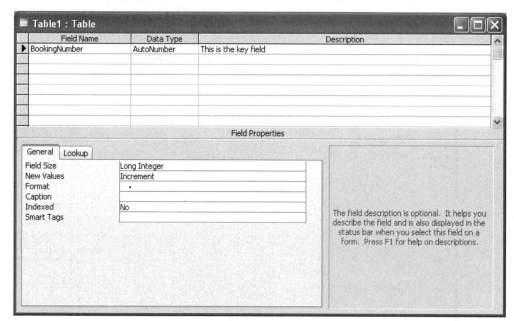

Figure 5.6: Defining field names and data types

Defining the primary key

- With the cursor still in the row for the BookingNumber, click the **Primary Key** button on the toolbar. The key symbol appears in the left-hand margin (termed the row selector) next to **BookingNumber**.

Entering other fields

Now we can enter all the other fields. Don't worry if you make a few mistakes – after all the fields are entered, you will learn how to move fields around, delete them or insert new fields. You can correct any mistakes at that point, and it'll be good practice.

> **Note:** A field name can be up to 64 characters long, can contain letters, numbers, spaces and other characters except for full-stops, exclamation marks and brackets.

- Enter the field name **Title** in the next row. Tab to the Data Type column and the default is **Text**, which is fine.

- In the next row, enter the field name **Initial**, and leave the field type in the next column as **Text**.

- Enter fields for **Surname**, **Address1**, **Address2**, **Postcode** and **Telephone**. All these fields have data type **Text**.

- Enter the field name **StartDate** and give it a data type of **Date/Time**.

- Enter the field name **EndDate** and give it a data type of **Date/Time**.

- Enter the field name **Cottage** and leave the data type as **Text**.

- Enter the field name **Deposit** and give it the data type **Currency**.

- Enter the field name **CleaningService** and give it the data type **Yes/No**.

- Enter the field name **NumberInParty** and give it the data type **Number**. In the **Field Properties** bottom half of the screen, you can choose what type of number you want the field to be by selecting from the Field Size drop-down list. Select **Byte** from this list. This allows a value of up to 255 to be entered.

Your table should now look like Figure 5.7.

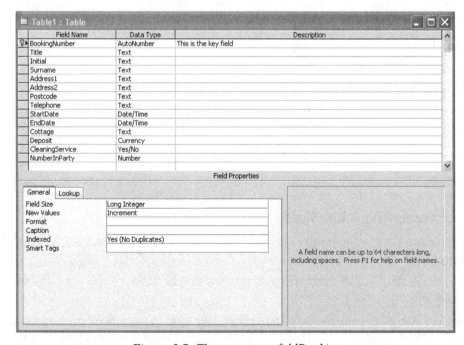

Figure 5.7: The structure of tblBooking

Saving the table structure

- Save the table structure by clicking the **Save** button or selecting **File, Save** from the menu bar. Don't worry if you have made some mistakes in the table structure – they can be corrected in a minute.

- You will be asked to type a name for your table. Type the name *tblBooking* and click **OK**.

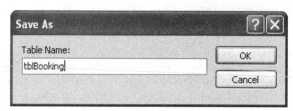

Figure 5.8: Saving and naming the table

- Click the **Close** icon in the top right-hand corner to close the window. You will be returned to the database window.

5.6   Editing a table structure

- In the Database window you will see that your new table is now listed.

> **Note:**   If you have named the table wrongly, or made a spelling mistake, right-click the name and select **Rename**. Then type in the correct name.

- Select the table name, click the **Design View** button and you are returned to *Design View*.

Inserting a field

To insert a new row for **Address3** just above **Postcode**:

- Click the row selector (the left-hand margin) for **Postcode**.

- Press the **Insert** key on the keyboard or click the **Insert Rows** button on the toolbar.

- Enter the new field name, *Address3*, data type **Text**.

Deleting a field

To delete the field you have just inserted:

- Select the field by clicking in its row selector.

- Press the **Delete** key on the keyboard or click the **Delete Rows** button on the toolbar.

If you make a mistake, you can use **Edit, Undo Delete** to restore the field.

Moving a field

- Click the row selector to the left of the field's name to select the field.

- Click again and drag to where you want the field to be. You will see a line appear between fields as you drag over them to indicate where the field will be placed.

Changing or removing a key field

- To change the key field to **Surname**, click the row selector for the **Surname** field and then click the **Primary Key** button on the toolbar.

- To remove the primary key altogether, select the row that is currently the key field and click the **Primary Key** button on the toolbar.

- Sometimes a primary key is made up of more than one field (a *composite* or *compound* key). Select the first field, hold down **Ctrl** and select the second field. Then click the **Primary Key** button.

When you have finished experimenting, restore **BookingNumber** as the primary key field of this table. Make any other necessary corrections to leave the fields as specified in Figure 5.1, and save the table structure.

Entering data in Datasheet view

It's time to enter some data. This can be done in Datasheet View.

- On the Toolbar, click the **Datasheet View** button.

The table now appears in Datasheet view as shown below.

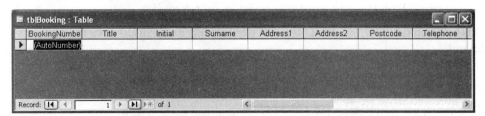

Figure 5.9: The empty table in Datasheet view

- You can drag the right border of the header (field name) of any field to alter its width. Drag the borders so that the whole row appears on the screen:

Figure 5.10: Field widths adjusted

- Enter the following records: (Sorry, no short cuts here!) Remember that Address has to be entered as 3 separate fields. **BookingNumber** will be added automatically by Access. ***Read the notes at the top of the next page before you start entering data.***

Title	Initial	Surname	Address	Telephone	StartDate	EndDate	Cottage	Deposit	Cleaning	Number InParty
Mr	A	Day	12 Field Lane Boston LA10 5TR	01372 245123	02/06/04	09/06/04	Elm	£250	Y	4
Mrs	M	Price	67 Church St Malden IP6 5EW	01876 987654	09/06/04	16/06/04	Holly	£300	Y	6
Mrs	P	May	The Old School Bramford IP8 3FD	01473 123987	16/06/04	23/06/04	Holly	£250	N	4
Ms	O	Dole	7 Birch Close Kingston KG5 3ES	01897 456789	09/06/04	16/06/04	Oak	£200	N	4
Mr	H	Mayhew	6 The Crescent Bath BA3 9JK	01394 200100	30/06/04	07/07/04	Elm	£200	N	2
Mr	K	Jones	23 Dales Rd Ipswich IP8 7HB	01473 556677	02/06/04	09/06/04	Oak	£300	N	6
Ms	B	Holder	9 Cherryfields Marston PE4 4NU	01723 303489	30/06/04	07/07/04	Oak	£300	Y	6
Miss	B	Sharpe	129 Melton Rd Leeds LE7 5TR	01882 447388	09/06/04	16/06/04	Elm	£250	N	6
Mrs	T	Butler	34 Bell Lane York YO7 3WS	01374 666543	02/06/04	09/06/04	Holly	£250	N	5

Figure 5.11: Sample data to be entered

67

> **Notes:** You can press **Tab** to move to the next field, or **Shift-Tab** to move to the previous field.
> You can't enter anything in the **BookingNumber** field – just tab to the next field and Access will automatically allocate the next number, starting with 1.
> Press the **Spacebar** or click the mouse button in the **CleaningService** column to put a tick in it
> You don't have to type the £ sign in the **Deposit** field – Access adds it automatically because you have specified the **Currency** field type.

- When you have entered all the data, click the **Close** icon in the top right corner of the current window. (Be careful to close just the Table window, not Access.)

- If you have changed column widths, you will be asked if you want to save the changes you made to the layout.

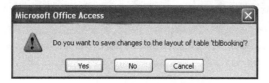

Figure 5.12: Saving changes to the Datasheet layout

- Click **Yes**. You will be returned to the Database window.

5.7   Editing, finding and deleting data in a table

- In the Database window, make sure that **Tables** is selected in the list of objects on the left of the window.

- Select **tblBooking** and click **Open**. This will open the table in Datasheet view. (If you wanted to change the actual structure of the table, for example to add a new field, you would select **Design**.)

Figure 5.13: Preparing to open tblBooking

The table appears as shown below:

Record selectors

Figure 5.14: tblBooking in Datasheet view

Moving to a particular record

You can move to a particular record using the **record selectors** in Datasheet view. Of course with so few records in the database it is quite easy to simply click in the required row, but you must remember that real databases usually have hundreds or thousands of records, so you may need these techniques one day.

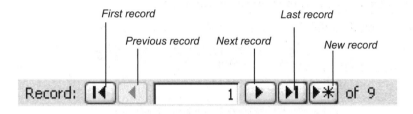

Figure 5.15: Using the record selectors

Finding a record

Sometimes you may want to find the record for a particular person or address. Again, this is most useful on a much larger database.

- Click the mouse anywhere in the **Surname** column.
- Suppose you want to find the record for Miss Sharpe.
- Click the **Find** button on the toolbar.

- Type the name *Sharpe* in the dialogue box, and click **Find Next**.

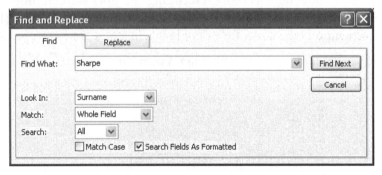

Figure 5.16: Finding a particular record

- You can use 'wildcards' such as * in a search. Try searching for **D***. This will find the next record starting with D each time you click **Find Next**.
- Close the Find and Replace window by clicking its **Close** icon.

Editing data

You can change the contents of any field (except the **BookingNumber** field, which being an **Autonumber** field, is set by Access) by clicking in the cell and editing in the normal way. Use the **Backspace** or **Delete** key to delete unwanted text and type in the corrections.

Remember you can undo changes using the **Undo** button.

Adding a new record

You can add a new record by clicking in the next blank line, and then typing the new record. With a large database, the easiest way to add a new record is to click the **New Record** button on either the record selector (see Figure 5.15) or on the menu bar. Then type the new record.

Deleting a record

To delete a record, click anywhere in the record that you want to delete and press the **Delete** button on the toolbar. You will see a message:

Figure 5.17: Confirming a record deletion

- Don't delete any of the original records you entered. Click **No**.
- If you have added or changed any records, restore them now to how they are in Figure 5.11. It does not matter if the **BookingNumber** field is different in your records.

5.8 Sorting records

You can perform a simple sort on one field by clicking anywhere in the column you want to sort on and pressing one of the two **Sort** buttons (**Sort Ascending** and **Sort Descending**) on the toolbar.

- Click in the **Surname** field and press the **Sort Ascending** button. The records will be sorted in ascending order of surname.
- Click in the **StartDate** column and press the **Sort Ascending** button. The records are rearranged in order of booking date.

You can sort on more than one field using **Records, Filter, Advanced Filter/Sort** from the menu. We will not go into this feature here.

5.9 Formatting and printing a datasheet

You can print a datasheet just as it is, or you can format it first by hiding unwanted columns, changing the order of the columns and changing column widths. We will practise these techniques.

- With **tblBooking** open in Datasheet view, click the **Print Preview** button. Your data appears as shown below:

Figure 5.18: The Datasheet in Print Preview mode

You will notice that the whole datasheet will not fit on one page in Portrait view. You can use the Page Selector at the bottom of the screen to look at the second page.

The **Print Preview** toolbar appears at the top of the screen. Using tools on this toolbar you can see both pages of the report. You can Zoom in on a page by clicking anywhere on it, or by clicking the **Zoom** button.

Click here to send to the printer

Click here to see two pages on screen

Click here to return to Design view

Figure 5.19: The Print Preview toolbar

- Click the **Close** button to return to Datasheet view.

Changing the Page layout

You can change the page layout to Landscape view.

- Select **File, Page Setup**… from the menu.
- Click the **Page** tab in the Page Setup dialog box. Click **Landscape**.

Figure 5.20: Changing the Page Setup to Landscape

- Try another Print Preview. This time it should fit on a single page.

Hiding and unhiding columns

Sometimes you may not want to print all the columns in the datasheet. You can hide the columns that you don't want.

- Make sure you have **tblBooking** on the screen in Datasheet view.
- Drag across the column headers from **Address1** to **Telephone**.
- From the menu select **Format, Hide Columns**. The columns will be hidden. (Note that to unhide columns, you select **Format, Unhide Columns**. There is no need to do this at the moment.)

Moving columns and adjusting column widths

Suppose you want to put the **Deposit** column right at the end.

- Click the **Deposit** column header to select the column.

- Click and hold down the mouse button in the header again, and drag it to the end of the table. The table should now appear as in Figure 5.21.

- Adjust the column widths by double-clicking in the column header on the border between each column. Your table should now appear as shown in Figure 5.21.

BookingN	Title	Initia	Surname	StartDate	EndDate	Cottage	CleaningService	NumberInParty	Deposit
9	Mrs	T	Butler	02/06/2004	09/06/2004	Holly	☐	5	£250.00
6	Mr	K	Jones	02/06/2004	09/06/2004	Oak	☐	6	£300.00
1	Mr	A	Day	02/06/2004	09/06/2004	Elm	☑	4	£250.00
8	Miss	B	Sharpe	09/06/2004	16/06/2004	Elm	☐	6	£250.00
4	Ms	O	Dole	09/06/2004	16/06/2004	Oak	☐	4	£200.00
2	Mrs	M	Price	09/06/2004	16/06/2004	Holly	☑	6	£300.00
3	Mrs	P	May	16/06/2004	23/06/2004	Holly	☐	4	£250.00
7	Ms	B	Holder	30/06/2004	07/07/2004	Oak	☑	6	£300.00
5	Mr	H	Mayhew	30/06/2004	07/07/2004	Elm	☐	2	£200.00
oNumber)							☐	0	£0.00

Figure 5.21: Columns hidden and the Deposit column moved to the end

- Click the **Print Preview** button again to see what the page will look like when printed out.

- Click the **Close** icon and click **Yes** when asked if you want to save the changes to the table layout.

5.10 Making queries

One of the most useful things you can do with a database is to find all records which satisfy certain criteria, such as *"Find all records for people who have booked a cleaning service"* or *"Find all records for Holly cottage bookings in June"*.

Creating a new query

- In the Database window, Click **Queries** in the list of objects on the left of the screen.

- Select either **Create query in Design view** or **Create query by using wizard** and click **New**. Either option takes you to the same dialogue box.

- In the next window, select **Design View**. Click **OK**. (See Figure 5.22 below.)

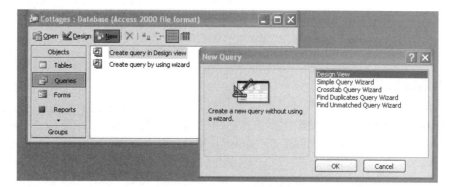

Figure 5.22: Creating a query in Design view

- In the Show Table dialogue box, click **Add** and then click **Close**.

Selecting fields to appear in the query

A query grid appears. You need to place selected fields onto the grid.

- In the **tblBooking** pane in the upper half of the window, double-click in turn the fields **Initial**, **Surname**, **StartDate**, **EndDate**, **Cottage**, **Deposit** and **CleaningService**. As you double-click, the fields will be placed in the query grid.

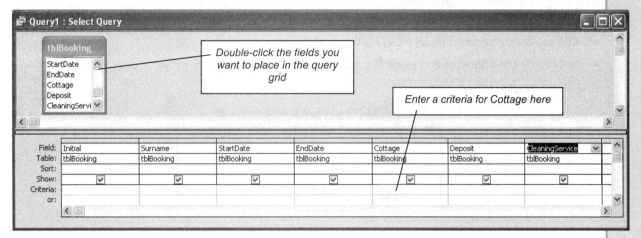

Figure 5.23: Putting fields into the Query grid

- If you want to remove a field from the query grid, click in the column header to select the column and press the **Delete** key.

- If you forget a field, for example **Cottage**, you can drag it from the **tblBooking** pane and put it on top of the next field on the right (**Deposit**). It will be inserted before this field.

Setting simple criteria

Now suppose you want to find all the bookings for Holly Cottage.

- In the **Cottage** column and **Criteria** row, enter "*Holly*". (You can type the quotes or omit them, in which case Access will add them automatically when you tab out of the field.)

- Now you can run your query to see the results. Click the **Run** button on the toolbar.

The results appear as shown below.

	Initial	Surname	StartDate	EndDate	Cottage	Deposit	CleaningService
▶	M	Price	09/06/2004	16/06/2004	Holly	£399.00	☑
	P	May	16/06/2004	23/06/2004	Holly	£250.00	☐
	T	Butler	02/06/2004	09/06/2004	Holly	£250.00	☐
*						£0.00	▣

Record: ◄ ◄ 1 ► ►I ►* of 3

Figure 5.24: The results of the query

Setting multiple criteria

You can use several different operators such as AND and OR in setting criteria. You can find all bookings for "Holly" OR "Elm", or all bookings for "Holly" which also require Cleaning Services.

It is easy to get confused between AND and OR – for example you may think that to find all bookings for both "Holly" and "Elm", we should use a criteria "Holly" AND "Elm". But the criteria refers to a single record, and no booking can be for both "Holly" and "Elm". That is why we need OR for this particular query.

In Access you do not have to use the operators AND and OR. You simply have to place multiple criteria on the same line to create an AND operator, and on different lines to create the OR operator.

- Return to Design view to change the query. (Don't close it.)

For example:

Suppose you wanted to find all the bookings for either Holly or Elm cottage. You will notice that the row under **Criteria** is headed **Or**.

- In the row headed **Or**, under the criteria "Holly", type "*Elm*".
- Run the query again.
- Now click the **Close** icon to close the query. You will be asked if you want to save it. Click **Yes**.
- Save it as **qryHolly&Elm**.

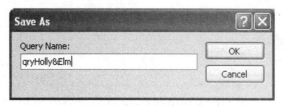

Figure 5.25: Saving a query

Using comparison operators

Sometimes you need to find all records with a field less than or greater than a particular value. You can use any of the following operators:

Operator	Meaning	Example	Finds (refer to Figure 5.18)
=	Equals	CleaningServices = Yes	Records 1, 2, 7
>	Greater than	Deposit>250	Records 2, 6,7
>=	Greater than or equal	Deposit >= £200	Records All
<	Less than	Surname<"Mayhew"	Records 1, 3, 4, 6, 7, 9
<=	Less than or equal	StartDate<=09/06/04	Records 1, 2, 4, 6, 8, 9
Between	Between, including both specified values	StartDate between 02/06/04 and 09/06/04	Records 1, 2, 4, 6, 8, 9

Figure 5.26: Comparison operators

The query shown in Figure 5.27 below finds all bookings for "Holly" or "Elm" with a StartDate between 02/06/04 and 09/06/04. (You do not have to type the # around the dates – Access adds this automatically.)

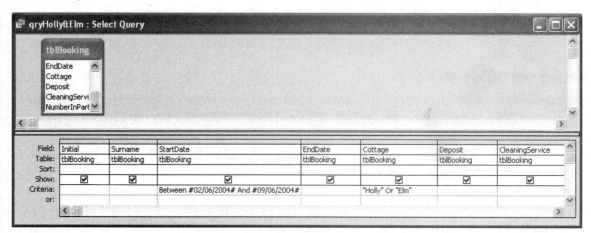

Figure 5.27: A query using multiple criteria

Sorting records and hiding fields

You can control certain aspects of the query result table, such as the sort order and which fields you want to see. For example you may want the results sorted by **Cottage**, and within **Cottage**, by **StartDate**.

- Open **qryHolly&Elm** in Design view.
- Click in the **Sort** row in the **Cottage** column and select **Ascending**.
- Run the query to see the result, noting that the records are not sorted in **StartDate** order and then return to Design view.
- Now click in the **Sort** row in the **StartDate** column and select **Ascending**.
- Run the query.

You will see that the records are now in **StartDate** sequence, but you really want them in **Cottage** sequence and THEN in **StartDate** sequence. By default Access uses the column order to decide the sort sequence, so you need to move the **Cottage** column to the left of the **StartDate** column.

- Return to Design view.
- Click in the **Cottage** column header.
- Click again and drag to the left of **StartDate**.

Suppose you decide you do not need the **Deposit** field in this particular report.

- Tick the **Show** box in the **Deposit** column to deselect it.
- Select **File, Save As** from the menu and save the amended query as **qryHolly&ElmSorted**.
- Run the query again. It should appear as in Figure 5.28

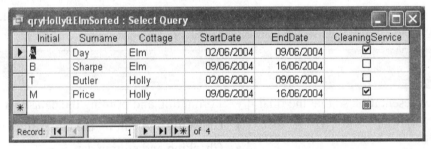

	Initial	Surname	Cottage	StartDate	EndDate	CleaningService
▶	A	Day	Elm	02/06/2004	09/06/2004	☑
	B	Sharpe	Elm	09/06/2004	16/06/2004	☐
	T	Butler	Holly	02/06/2004	09/06/2004	☐
	M	Price	Holly	09/06/2004	16/06/2004	☑
∗						

Figure 5.28: Selected records sorted

- You can do a Print Preview by clicking the **Print Preview** button. The page layout can be altered as you did in paragraph 5.9.
- Close the query, and then close the database.

There is a lot more to learn about Access but you've made a good start!

5.11 Relating this chapter to the specification

Specification Reference (Part B)	What you have done to satisfy this
IT2.1	
Select information relevant to the tasks	• Interview with owner of cottages • Planning process • Selecting field properties and data types • Extracting information from paper records • Designing the database
IT2.2	
Enter and combine information using formats that help development	• Use of tables • Entering records • Formatting the datasheet • Field properties and formats
Develop information and derive new information as appropriate	• Adding, deleting, editing records • Sorting records • Queries on the database using multiple criteria • Hiding fields
IT2.3	
Develop the presentation so that the final output is accurate and shows consistent use of formats	• Formatting and printing the datasheet • Checking and editing the table structure • Checking and editing data • Saving the file
Use layout appropriate to the types of information	• Database meets requirements of cottage owner

5.12 Evidence for your portfolio

The table below shows the evidence that you should include for a typical database project. You need to find a database application to develop, and collect the evidence as you go along.

Be careful not to choose a database application which is too complex. Choose one which involves only a single 'entity' such as people, videos or books in a personal collection, animals or birds, cars, etc. Do not try to develop a database for a library or a video hire shop, say, which requires you to have related tables for books/videos and borrowers, unless you have studied more about databases than is found in this chapter. Some suitable ideas include:

♦ A database of cars or houses for sale, from which the user can look up records satisfying criteria such as a price range

♦ A database of members of an organisation such as a Scout group, showing what subscriptions are due, type of member, and personal details

♦ A database of sports fixtures giving dates, opposing teams, results, etc.

♦ A database of players in a tennis or squash club showing personal details, position in league, etc.

Type of evidence	✔
A brief written description of the activity	
Notes of the interview with the user	
Printouts of field properties and formats	
Working drafts of datasheets annotated with amendments to be made and why	
Notes of queries to be generated and why	
Screenshots of data validation in action	
Screenshots from Explorer to show the saved file	
Final printouts of unsorted and sorted datasheets and queries	
Record from your assessor of how you developed the content and presentation of your work	

5.13 Sample questions

A gardener keeps the following database of the plants in his garden.

NAME	TYPE	COLOUR	HEIGHT	PLANTING DATE
Bellis	Biennial	Mixed	15cm	18.05.2004
Aster	Annual	Mixed	60cm	16.03.2004
Salvia	Annual	Red	45cm	03.06.2004
Forget-me-not	Biennial	Blue	20cm	14.09.2004
Begonia	Perennial	Pink	30cm	11.03.2004
Godetia	Annual	Pink	30cm	30.05.2004
Peony	Perennial	Pink	60cm	02.02.2004

1. This database has
    A   5 fields and 8 records
    B   8 fields and 5 records
    C   5 fields and 7 records
    D   7 fields and 5 records

2. To find all perennial plants requires a
    A   search for TYPE >= Perennial
    B   search for "Perennial" = TYPE
    C   search for TYPE = "Perennial"
    D   alphabetical sort on COLOUR

3. Annual plants that were planted out after 06.04.04 can be found by
    A   TYPE = "Annual" AND PLANTING DATE < "06.04.2004"
    B   TYPE = "Annual" AND PLANTING DATE > "06.04.2004"
    C   TYPE = "Annual" OR PLANTING DATE > "06.04.2004"
    D   TYPE = "Annual" OR PLANTING DATE = "06.04.200"

4. To obtain a list of plants in order of TYPE and then NAME, you must
    A   sort on NAME and then TYPE
    B   sort on TYPE only
    C   sort on NAME only
    D   sort on TYPE and then NAME

5. The entries displayed in the NAME column are of type
    A   text
    B   logical
    C   numeric
    D   conditional

6. When the database is searched for all pink perennial plants, the following number of records will be found
    A   none
    B   one
    C   two
    D   three

Chapter 6 – Finding, Selecting and Sharing Information

Objectives

❑ To identify sources of information to use in IT activities

❑ To learn how to get the most from the Internet

❑ To use CD-ROMs for reference

❑ To appreciate the importance of acknowledging your sources

❑ To learn how to share information via e-mail

6.1   Sources of Information

An important part of the IT Key Skills qualification at all levels is the development of skills for searching and selecting appropriate source information. For example, you may need to find the temperatures for a particular city over a period of time for a spreadsheet activity like the one in Chapter 3. Or, you may need to collect together some information to compile a newsletter as in Chapter 12. You will also find the research methods described in this chapter useful in your main area of study.

There are a number of sources and investigative methods that can be used for researching this kind of information.

♦ **Primary** Sources. Using primary sources involves talking directly to the people involved or going directly to the situation to examine it at first hand (for example, interviewing the holiday cottage owner in Chapter 5).

♦ **Secondary** Sources. Using secondary sources involves finding and studying sources that have already been recorded. This includes the Internet, CD-ROMs, books, back copies of newspapers etc.

The main sources that you are likely to consider for the types of activity described in this book include the following:

♦ The Internet

♦ CD-ROMs

♦ Books, newspapers and magazines

♦ People

At level 3 you must ensure that your portfolio evidence includes at least one example of using IT to search for information and one example of a non-IT based information source. Your evidence must also demonstrate that you have sent and received e-mails, one of which should have an attachment – this is dealt with later in this chapter.

It is essential that you keep a record of all the research sources that you use for an activity. The Information Seeking record sheet (provided at www.payne-gallway.co.uk/ksit) could be used for this purpose. Once completed, it must be filed in your portfolio along with the other evidence for that particular activity.

6.2 The Internet

The Internet is a vast system that connects people and information through computers. By using the Internet you can look up information on any subject you can imagine.

The World Wide Web (WWW) has been developed to make it easy for anyone to access and view documents that are stored on computers anywhere on the Internet.

Web Sites are the pages you visit as you travel around the WWW. Every Web Site consists of one or more documents called pages. An important feature of **web pages** is their capability to contain **hyperlinks** (sometimes referred to as **hotspots**). These are links to another page or location on the WWW. Both text and graphics can be set up as hyperlinks. A **home page** is the first page of a web site that the user sees. It serves as an introduction to the web site.

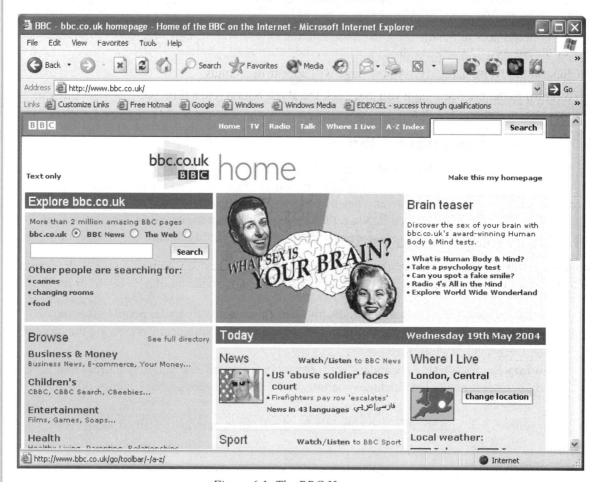

Figure 6.1: The BBC Home page

Every page has its own unique name or address, called a **Uniform Resource Locator (URL)**. When you type a URL it is important that you type it with every dot, slash and colon in the right place.

Figure 6.2: A Uniform Resource Locator (URL)

A **web browser** is a software package you use to view information from the Internet. A browser program, like Internet Explorer or Netscape Navigator, acts as a go-between for your computer and the WWW.

6.3   Accessing a known web site

- Start Internet Explorer by clicking the icon on the Quick Launch toolbar (next to the Windows **Start** button). Alternatively, select it from the **Programs** list from the **Start** menu.
- You may be asked if you wish to connect to the Internet. Click **Yes**.
- Click inside the address box.
- When the URL in the address box appears highlighted, type *www.bbc.co.uk*.
- Click the **Go** button.

After a few seconds the BBC home page appears on your screen.

- Move your pointer around the text and graphics on the BBC home page. The mouse arrow changes to the shape of a hand as it passes over hyperlinks on the page. Usually hyperlinks appear as underlined coloured text or graphics (the default is to display text links in blue before they are clicked. As soon as they are clicked they change to purple).
- Click on the **News** category. A new page will appear in seconds.
- To return to the previous page you can click the **Back** button (each time you click the **Back** or **Forward** button on the Internet Explorer toolbar, you are returned to the page you viewed previously during your current browsing session).

6.4   Searching for information

There are plenty of search tools available to help you find the pages you want on the WWW. These tools all work in roughly the same way; you form a search query made up of a keyword or phrase, and the search tool looks through its database of documents on the Internet. It then returns a list of documents that match. Each match is called a hit and contains a hyperlink to the corresponding web page.

There are several different types of search tool – the ones you are likely to use most are search engines and site directories.

Search engines

Robotically built indexes or search engines send electronic crawlers (sometimes called trawlers, spiders, worms or robots) through the Web looking for pages and then return the findings. However, just because they cannot find it does not mean it is not there. It just means the crawlers haven't visited that site yet. Each engine can only return its crawler's latest findings.

Examples of search engines include:

- www.google.com
- www.altavista.co.uk
- www.hotbot.co.uk
- www.lycos.co.uk
- www.webcrawler.com
- www.ask.co.uk

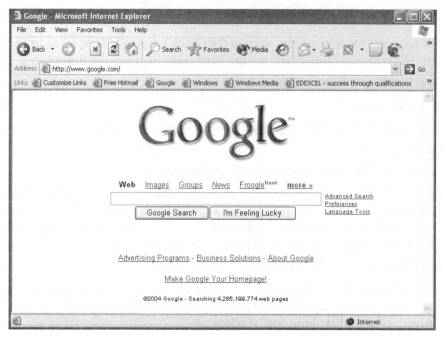

Figure 6.3: The Google search engine

Site directories

These sort sites into categories of subject, date, platform or even level of 'coolness'. To move around a site directory, you generally click the links to each category and subcategory until you find what you are looking for. You can also use a keyword search to find specific sites. Directories often include some form of review or comment about the site.

Examples of site directories include:

- http://uk.yahoo.com
- http://yahooligans.yahoo.com
- www.ukdirectory.co.uk
- www.dmoz.org

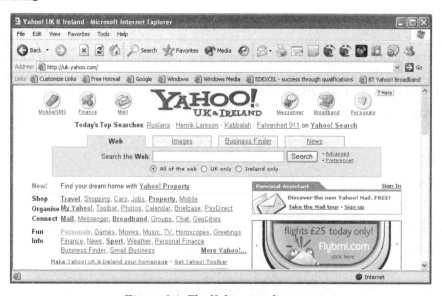

Figure 6.4: The Yahoo site directory

Keyword searches

You must take some care in setting up your search query to communicate exactly what you want to find. Remember these useful tips:

- If possible do not use connecting words like *the* and *an*.
- Check your spelling.
- Be specific.
- Try a few different word combinations.
- Run your search using at least two different search tools.

Most search tools allow you to refine a search by using advanced search facilities. For example you can request that certain pages are excluded by adding a keyword with a minus in front. Similarly if you are particularly interested in a topic, you can add keywords with a plus in front. For example if you want to find web pages concerned with double-glazed windows, you could narrow down the search with the following search criteria:

> *windows -Microsoft +double-glazing*

Some logical operators are also supported. For example to find details of holidays in London or Rome, you could enter the following:

> *holiday London OR Rome*

6.5 Adding a page to Favorites

To save having to remember how to return to a particular web page you can **bookmark** it by adding it to a list of favourite sites.

- Go back to the BBC home page.
- From the menu bar choose **Favorites**, **Add to Favorites** and click **OK**.

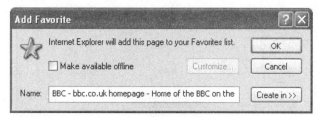

Figure 6.5: Adding to Favorites

To return to a 'Favorite' page:

- Click the **Favorites** button on the toolbar.
- Click the item in the Favorites pane on the left to bring up that page.
- Click the **Favorites** button again to hide the pane.

6.6 Storing information

Once you have found the exact page you have been looking for you may want to print the page, save the whole page or copy part of the information and save it.

Printing a web page

Remember that web pages have no logical end and you often have to scroll down the screen to move to the bottom of a page. That page might translate into several printed pages. The procedure for printing from Internet Explorer is very similar to printing from other Windows programs such as

Word. Clicking the **Print** button on the Standard toolbar sends the onscreen page to the printer. For more control over various options, use the **Print** command from the **File** menu. If the page you wish to print contains frames (multiple rectangular sections, each with its own function and look), you will find an additional **Print Frames** option on the **Print Dialogue** box.

Many sites now offer a special printable version that has fewer graphics and less formatting.

Saving a web page

Internet Explorer will allow you to save any web page to the hard drive of your computer or to a floppy disk. The saved page is just like any other Windows document so you can open the browser and view the page while you are working offline.

- Open Internet Explorer, connect to the Internet and find a web page that you want to save.
- With the page you want visible on the screen, choose **Save as** from the **File** menu. The **Save Web Page** dialogue box appears as shown below.
- Navigate to the folder in which you want to store your saved documents.
- Enter a filename.
- Make sure that **Web Page, Complete (*.htm,*.html)** appears in the **Save As Type** box.
- Click **Save**.

Figure 6.6: Saving a web page

- To view the saved web page, open Internet Explorer and work offline.
- Choose **Open** from the **File** menu.
- Use the **Browse** button to navigate to the folder where you saved the web page.

Figure 6.7: Finding a saved web page

> **Note:** You will find that Internet Explorer creates a new folder with the same name as the saved web page, but with **_files** added. This new folder holds files containing the web page graphics.

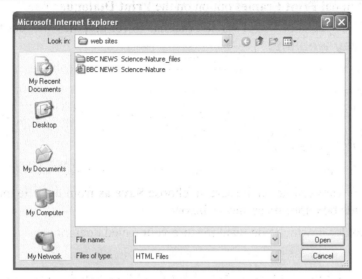

Figure 6.8: Opening a saved web page

- Select the named file with the Internet Explorer symbol.
- Click **Open**.
- Click **OK** on the Open dialogue box.

Copying and saving selected parts of a web page

The easiest way to do this is to copy the text from the web page in Internet Explorer and paste into a new Word document.

- Open a new document in Word.
- Open Internet Explorer, connect to the Internet, and find the web page that you want.
- Select the text on the web page and click **Copy** from the **Edit** menu.
- Click on the new Word document on the task bar to bring it onto the screen.
- Click **Paste** from the **Edit** menu.
- Save the new Word document and disconnect from the Internet.

6.7   Transferring files

Your web browser can do more than just bring web pages to your computer. It can also be used to download files from the Internet for you to use at a later time. Some of the different types of files you can download include:

- Install programs (such as games). These files normally have the **.exe** suffix after the filename.
- Multimedia files. These include files that play music, video or produce sounds. Your computer needs to be equipped with the appropriate sound card, speakers etc. to be able to play these files.
- Documents in many formats. Sometimes you need a special reader to view these files. For example PDF format, often used for downloadable files, requires the Adobe Acrobat reader.
- Upgrades and drivers. Manufacturers often offer upgrades to existing files on your computer. Drivers can be obtained from manufacturers' sites for many devices such as printers.

Sometimes large files are compressed to make them smaller and quicker to download. These need to be decompressed before they can be used. One of the most popular compression programs is WinZip. Often the downloadable files will be automatically decompressed after downloading (these are called self-extracting files). If they do not you will require a program such as WinZip to decompress the file.

The Payne-Gallway web site

For a number of the activities in this book we have provided downloadable files on our web site.

These files have normally been compressed in groups into one smaller file. For example to complete the Newsletter activity in Chapter 12, you download the file **kschap12.exe**. This file must be decompressed once you have downloaded it and a total of twelve files will be stored on your hard drive. The procedure to download this type of file is as follows:

- Go to the www.payne-gallway.co.uk/ksit page on the Payne-Gallway web site.
- Click on the link to download **KSChap12.exe**.
- You will be asked if you wish to run the file from its current location or save it to disk. Select the **Save** option.

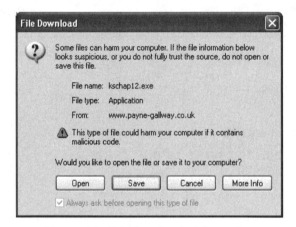

Figure 6.9: File download dialogue box

As the file downloads the following progress box will be displayed.

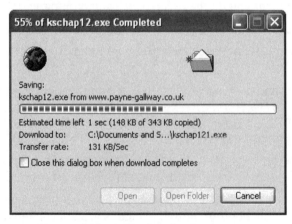

Figure 6.10: A file download in progress

You will then see a dialogue box confirming that the file has been saved.

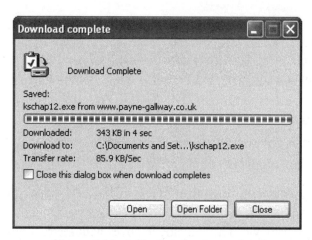

Figure 6.11: A file download completed

- Note where the file has been downloaded to and click **Open** (you can disconnect from the Internet at this point).

- You will then be asked to unzip the files to a given location. Use the **Browse** button to change the location if you wish.

- Click **Unzip**.

- Use Windows Explorer to check the location of the unzipped files.

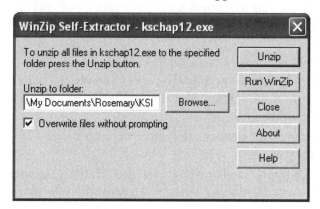

Figure 6.12: WinZip self-extractor dialogue box

6.8 CD-ROMs

CD-ROMs (Compact Disk Read Only Memory) may carry text, pictures, sound and video digitally, which can be loaded on to the CD-ROM drive of a computer. These disks can store large amounts of information such as books and magazines. For example, encyclopaedias like Encyclopaedia Britannica and Encarta are now available on disk. Searches can be made to find specific information and the results called up not only in text but also in picture and sound form. There is no interactive capability with these disks, but they do help to visualise a topic and offer examples of distinctive sounds.

To install CD-ROMs is very simple. Most automatically run a Setup program when you insert them into the CD-ROM drive of your computer. If this does not happen do the following:

- From the Windows **Start** menu, click **Run**.

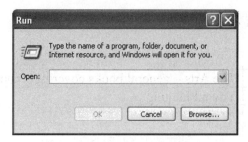

Figure 6.13: Running a program

- In the **Run** dialogue box, click on **Browse** to find the CD-ROM drive (often D: or E:) and click on the Setup file for the program.

- The Setup program will display different dialogue boxes with instructions to guide you through the installation.

- When you come to run the program, you will find that the CD-ROM must be inserted in the machine as all the reference files are not installed on your computer.

On screen instructions will then be given to guide you round the program and show you, for example, where to enter a search query.

6.9 Books

Technological advances have brought enormous potential with CD-ROMs and the Internet, but reference books can still be of tremendous value and our library system and their staff can be a great help to you.

Most public, school and college libraries use a system of arranging non-fiction books invented by Melvil Dewey, an American librarian, in 1876. The system is referred to as the **Dewey Decimal Classification Scheme**. It is useful to know how this system works, and it may save you time when searching for a book on a particular subject.

According to the Dewey system, all books on the same subject are found in the same place, with books on similar subjects nearby.

Each subject is allocated a 3-figure number which can be extended by adding a decimal point and then more numbers – the longer the number after the decimal point, the more detailed the subject.

First of all, knowledge is divided up into 10 main sections as follows:

Section Number	Subjects included
000	General: encyclopaedias, directories, books of facts and records, computers
100	Philosophy and psychology: books about ideas, thinking and the mind
200	Religion: religions and beliefs
300	Social issues: books about how society works and functions
400	Languages
500	Science: maths, astronomy, physics, chemistry, nature, plants, birds, animals, the weather
600	Technology: machines and inventions, electronics, medicine and the human body, farming, pets, food and cookery
700	The Arts: drawing, painting, photography, music, dance, theatre, hobbies, sport
800	Literature: poems, plays and critical works
900	History and countries: including explorers and biographies

Figure 6.14: Dewey 10 main sections

Each of the main divisions is then divided into ten as follows:

Section Number	Subjects included
700	The Arts – general books covering a number of arts
710	Town Planning
720	Architecture
730	Sculpture
740	Drawing/Decorative arts
750	Painting and paintings
760	Printing and graphic arts
770	Photography
780	Music
790	Theatre, games, sport

Figure 6.15: Dewey subdivisions

Each of these more general divisions is then divided up again, to allow for easier location of more specific topics, for example:

Section Number	Subjects included
730	Sculpture
731	Process, forms and subjects of sculpture
732	Sculpture up to 500 AD
733	Greek, Etruscan and Roman sculpture
734	Sculpture from *c*.500 to 1399 AD
735	Sculpture from 1400
736	Carving and carvings
737	Coins
738	Ceramic arts
739	Art metalwork

Figure 6.16: Further Dewey subdivisions

These subjects can then become even more specific by adding a decimal point and more numbers, for example:

Section Number	Subjects included
738.1	Ceramics and pottery
738.2	Porcelain

Figure 6.17: Specific subject areas

The more numbers after the decimal point, the more specific the subject. Fortunately you do not have to remember all these numbers. All libraries have subject indexes which are generally alphabetical lists of subjects with their numbers.

Most libraries now have computer systems installed, many of which provide Internet access. They can be used to search the library database for a particular book. Searches can often be made on Title, Author, ISBN number or Keyword. The results of the search give information on the book's status (e.g. if it is on loan, available for loan etc.) and also its Dewey decimal number so that you can find it easily.

6.10 Newspapers and magazines

It is important that any research material that you use is not only accurate, but also up-to-date. Newspapers are an ideal source for the latest updates on news items. They employ journalists who specialise in certain areas and often include one-off features about a particular topic. You also need to look out for special supplements that the broadsheet newspapers publish regularly; for example The Guardian has a Media section on Mondays.

Public, school and college libraries usually stock back copies of the more popular broadsheet newspapers. These cannot normally be taken out on loan but used for reference whilst you are in the library.

Several of the newspapers now have on-line versions available on the WWW, for example:

www.guardian.co.uk

www.dailytelegraph.co.uk

www.sunday-times.co.uk

www.independent.co.uk

www.observer.co.uk

Back copies of several newspapers, for example The Guardian and The Sunday Times, are also available on CD-ROM.

Specialist magazines often have in-depth articles about particular topics. Once again, most libraries keep back copies of a selection of titles which can be used for reference purposes.

Figure 6.18: The Guardian on-line

6.11 People

Primary sources of information can be some of the most interesting, but you clearly need to have access to the person or situation under consideration.

Personal Interviews

It is a good idea to plan some of the questions beforehand, so that you make best use of the time. Then keep the following points in mind:

♦ Look at the person when they are talking to you.

♦ Keep your mind on the topic of conversation.

♦ Do not always insist on having the last word.

♦ Ensure the interviewee is comfortable.

♦ Be sensitive to a speaker's need for privacy.

♦ Be sensitive to the speaker's tone of voice and 'body language'.

Telephone Interviews

Interviewing over the telephone can save time and money, but you have to be even more sensitive to the feelings of the interviewee. Remember you may be interrupting them at a busy time, so always be as polite and brief as possible.

Figure 6.19: Be as brief as possible!

Personal Observation

If you are writing a review of a football match for a newsletter item, the readers will expect you to have actually seen the event. If you have observed an event you do not have to rely on other people's views or information, and you can add extra detail that you think is important.

Taking Photographs

A good photograph can support and give emphasis to written, factual information. It can often be difficult to find a photograph that someone else has taken that is appropriate and not subject to copyright, so taking your own can solve both of these problems.

Digital cameras are now more readily available. These allow you to take photographs which are stored in the camera's memory. The camera is then connected directly to the computer and a software package downloads the pictures onto your hard drive. These software packages often allow you to edit the photographs so that you can, for example, crop the picture and enlarge just one area of it.

Another option is to take a photograph with an ordinary camera, get the film developed and then scan the pictures into your computer. Again the software scanning packages often allow some photo-editing.

6.12 Acknowledging your sources

The Association of Colleges define plagiarism as "the presentation of someone else's work, ideas, opinions or discoveries, whether published or not, as one's own".

Increased access to the Internet means that many more people can download or copy material from the WWW. It is much easier to copy some text from a web page and paste it into your own document than it is to copy large chunks out of a book. But do not be tempted! All schools and colleges will have disciplinary procedures to deal with these problems.

Researching some information using the methods described in this chapter means you are drawing on other people's ideas. You must not copy text unless you quote someone, in which case you must use quote marks and attribute the quote to them (as in the first paragraph of this section).

An easy way of acknowledging your sources is to use a list of references. This adds validity to the information and allows others to check and assess your sources.

Both you and your teacher will be required to sign declarations confirming that the work you have submitted for assessment in your portfolio is your own. If you have worked in a group for some activities it must be easy to identify the individual contribution of each group member.

6.13 Sharing information via e-mail

The portfolio evidence you submit must show at least one example of using e-mail. At Level 3 the e-mail must have an attachment. One way of doing this would be to use e-mail to send drafts of your documents to another student, a member of staff or a user. You do this by creating a new message and attaching the file(s). A program which is often used to handle e-mail is Microsoft Outlook Express which comes with Internet Explorer.

- Click the **Outlook Express** icon near the **Start** button, or alternatively select **Start**, **Programs**, **Outlook Express**.

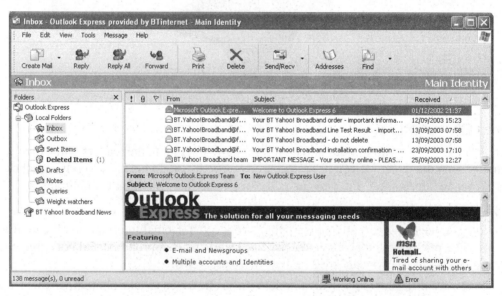

Figure 6.20: Preparing to send or receive e-mail using Outlook Express

To send a new message to someone you obviously need to know their e-mail address. E-mail addresses are quite like web site addresses and are made up in much the same way. An e-mail address has no spaces, is usually all in lower case letters and always contains an @ character. Every e-mail address is unique and must be entered correctly or the message will come back undelivered.

- Click on the **Create Mail** button on the toolbar.

The New Message window opens.

- Type the address in the **To:** box.

- Leave the **Cc:** box blank. This is used if you want to send a copy of the message to someone else.

- Type something in the **Subject:** box to say what the message is about.

- Type a message in the main window (the message box) telling the recipient you have attached a document.

- Click the **Attach** button on the toolbar.

- In the Insert Attachment window, navigate to the file and click **Attach**.

- Click on **Send** in the New e-mail window to send the message.

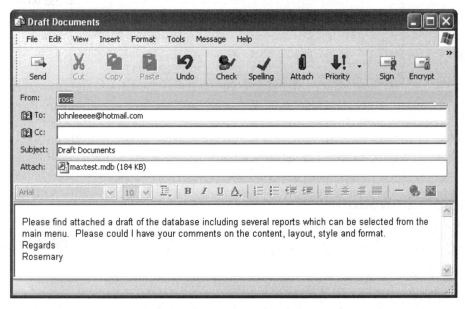

Figure 6.21: Sending an e-mail with an attachment

Your colleague may send the document back to you as an e-mail attachment. If you receive a message with an attachment, the message header has a paperclip icon beside it.

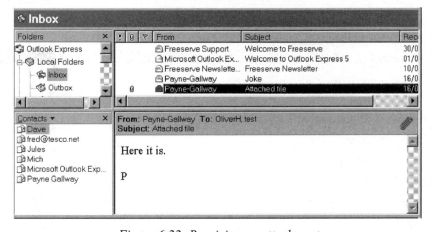

Figure 6.22: Receiving an attachment

You must then save the attachment to disk, otherwise when you delete the message you will delete the attachment too. The default folder for saving attachments is **Windows\Desktop** but you can change this with the **Browse** button.

- Choose **File**, **Save Attachments**.

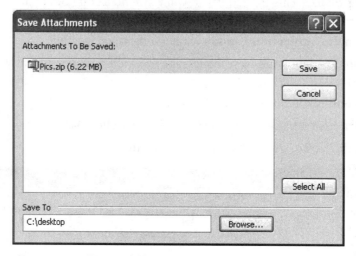

Figure 6.23: Saving an attachment

- Click **Save**.
- Double-click the attached file's icon to open it.

6.14 Sample questions

You are asked to find out about the Natural History Museum in London.

1. What IT source would you use to find out this information?

    A   Internet

    B   A floppy disk

    C   Digital camera

    D   Zip drive

2. What tool would you use to search for this information?

    A   A scanner

    B   A search engine

    C   The control panel

    D   FTP software

3. Which of these is an example of a web browser?

    A   Microsoft Excel

    B   Internet Explorer

    C   Yahoo

    D   A database package

Chapter 7 – Working with IT

Objectives

- ❑ To identify errors and their causes
- ❑ To consider copyright and software licensing
- ❑ To consider the safety and security of equipment, the user and data

7.1 Identifying errors

It is surprising how quickly PC users start to depend on their computer systems and how frustrating it can be when things go wrong. Here are some basic things you can try if you get a problem:

- Check that the PC and all its peripherals (e.g. screen, keyboard, mouse, printer, speakers etc.) are all plugged in and switched on.
- Check the power supply for a blown fuse.
- Check that all cables are in place.
- If you were unable to shut your computer down correctly, when you restart it a program called **Scandisk** will run to check your hard disk for damage. If the scan finds any problem it will tell you if it can be repaired.
- If your screen freezes up so that you cannot use your keyboard or mouse, you can try to find out which program is causing the problem:
- Press **Ctrl-Alt-Del** (all at the same time) on the keyboard to display **Task Manager**.

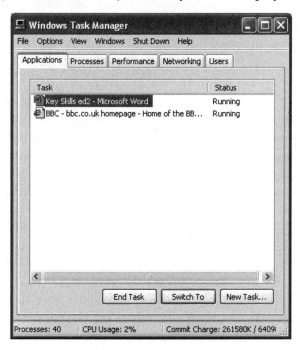

Figure 7.1: Task Manager

- Any program whose status is **Not Responding** may be at fault. Click the name of the program and click **End Task** to close it.

This should close down the faulty program and allow you to carry on working. If it doesn't, click **Shut Down** – this will close your PC down safely and is always better than hitting the **Reset** button.

- Read the manual. The chances are that the full manual will probably be an electronic file rather than a printed document. It may have been installed on your PC or you might find it on your installation CD-ROM.

- Visit the manufacturer's web site. It may be that the problem you are experiencing is well known and that a cure is already available. This may be in the form of a downloadable software 'patch'.

- Contact your technical support team. This may be available in the school or college where you study or may be provided by the manufacturer of your PC if you are working at home. Always make sure you have details of the PC to hand, together with exact details of the problem, the sequence of events leading up to the error and any error messages that have been displayed.

7.2   Copyright

Computer software is copyright material – that means it is protected in the UK by the Copyright, Designs and Patents Act 1988. It is owned by the software producer and it is illegal to make unauthorised copies.

When you buy software it is often supplied in a sealed package (e.g. CD-ROM case) on which the terms and conditions of sale are printed. This is called the software licence and when the user opens the package they are agreeing to abide by the licence terms.

Software licences usually permit the user to use one copy on any single computer. It is considered to be in use if it is loaded into either the computer's temporary memory (RAM) or onto the hard disk drive. With network licences the software is often loaded onto the file server and the licence specifies how many users on the network can access it at any one time.

It is illegal to make copies of the software, except for backup purposes, so you are breaking the law if you copy some software from a friend to use on your own computer.

Data that is held on computer is often subject to copyright. For example not everyone has the ability or opportunity to draw or to take photographs and you often want to include copies of someone else's work in your documents. These images may well be copyright and belong to the original artist or photographer. If this is the case it may be possible to contact the publisher for permission to use the material, but this can be a lengthy process. To be outside the copyright law, the artist/photographer/writer has to have been dead for 70 years. If this is the case and you would like to use, for example, some old photographs, you may do so freely, but it is often best to acknowledge the source somewhere in your document.

7.3   Safety and security of equipment

It is important that organisations consider general security issues in order to guard against the theft of computer equipment:

- Some organisations employ security staff or CCTV systems to monitor access to their facilities.
- Staff may be issued with passes with their photographs on. These cards often store the user's ID on the magnetic strip on the back, and a computer program will check this and authorise access when the card is swiped through a reader. Visitors are issued with temporary cards so

that their movements may be monitored. This kind of system is also useful in the case of an evacuation as it is easy to ascertain who is on site at the time.

♦ A visitor's log book is a simpler way of recording this type of information.

♦ Doors can also be secured for entry through the use of a code entered by pressing a certain sequence of buttons on a keypad. Only authorised personnel are given the code.

♦ Equipment can also be marked with special infra-red codes or have the postcode stamped on them to ensure return to its rightful owner if it is stolen. The theft of processors and memory from computers has risen over the past few years. This has led some organisations (for example colleges) to remove these components when the equipment is not in use.

♦ New staff are often introduced to simple routine security procedures such as closing windows and locking doors at the end of the day, always wearing their security pass and generally being alert to strangers in the building. All of these common-sense measures can help reduce the level of theft from organisations.

7.4   Safety of the user

Computers and health

Computers can be held responsible for a whole raft of health problems, from eyestrain to wrist injuries, back problems to foetal abnormalities, stomach ulcers to mental collapse. Articles appear regularly in the newspapers relating stories of employees who are suing their employers for computer-related illnesses.

Not so long ago it was thought that the widespread use of these fantastic machines, that could perform calculations and process data with lightning speed and complete accuracy, would free up humans to work maybe only two or three hours a day, while the computer did the lion's share. In fact, people seem to be working harder than ever, trying to keep up with the output of their computers. Human beings are the weak link in the chain, needing food, rest, a social life; prone to headaches, stress, tired limbs and mistakes.

Figure 7.2: Stress at work

Stress

Stress is often a major factor in work-related illness. Simply thinking about computers is enough to cause stress in some people. It is stressful to be asked to perform tasks which are new to you and which you are not sure you can cope with. It is stressful to know that you have more work to do than you can finish in the time available. It is stressful, even, to have too little to do and to be bored all day.

The introduction of computers into the workplace can have detrimental effects on the well-being of information workers at many different levels in an organisation. For example:

♦ Some companies may use computers to monitor their workers' productivity, which often increases their stress levels. Symptoms include headaches, stomach ulcers and sleeplessness.

♦ Many people are afraid of computers and fear that they will not be able to learn the new skills required, or that their position of seniority will be undermined by younger 'whiz kids' with a high level of competence in IT.

♦ It can be almost impossible for some people to get away from work. Pagers, mobile phones, laptop computers and modems mean that even after leaving the office, there is no need to stop work – indeed, should you even *think* of stopping work? As a busy executive, can you afford to waste 45 minutes on the train to Ipswich reading the newspaper or just gazing out of the window, when you could be tap-tap-tapping on your laptop, or infuriating your fellow passengers by holding long and boring conversations on your mobile phone?

♦ 'Information overload' means that managers are often bombarded with far more information than they can assimilate, producing 'information anxiety'. Try typing the words 'Information Overload' into one of the World Wide Web's search engines and within seconds, it will have searched millions of information sources all over the world and come up with thousands of references all pre-sorted so that those most likely to be of interest are at the top.

♦ A survey of 500 heads of IT departments revealed that over three quarters of respondents had suffered from failing personal relationships, loss of appetite, addiction to work and potential alcohol abuse. The continuing developments within IT ensure that it is always in the minds of business executives and also that it is blamed for most corporate problems. The very speed of development, for which IT is now famous, and the need to keep pace with this is also a major contributing factor to IT stress-related illness.

Repetitive Strain Injury (RSI)

RSI is the collective name for a variety of disorders affecting the neck, shoulders and upper limbs. It can result in numbness or tingling in the arms and hands, aching and stiffness in the arms, neck and shoulders, and an inability to lift or grip objects. Some sufferers cannot pour a cup of tea or type a single sentence without excruciating pain.

The Health and Safety Executive say that more than 100,000 workers suffer from RSI.

Eyestrain

Computer users are prone to eyestrain from spending long hours in front of a screen. Many computer users prefer a dim light to achieve better screen contrast, but this makes it difficult to read documents on the desk. A small spotlight focussed on the desktop can be helpful. There is no evidence that computer use causes permanent damage to the eyes, but glare, improper lighting, improperly corrected vision (through not wearing the correct prescription glasses), poor work practices and poorly designed workstations all contribute to temporary eyestrain.

Extremely low frequency (ELF) radiation

In normal daily life we are constantly exposed to ELF radiation not only from electricity mains and computer monitors but also naturally occurring sources such as sunshine, fire and the earth's own magnetic field. Research into the effects of ELF radiation is increasing and seems to indicate that it may be connected to some health problems. Several studies have tried to establish whether there is a link between monitor use and problems in pregnancy such as early miscarriages. The results are not clear-cut, because although some studies seem to show a correlation between an increased rate of miscarriages and long hours spent at a VDU in the first trimester of pregnancy, other factors such as stress and poor ergonomic conditions could have played a part.

Computers, health and the law

Occupational health and safety legislation in Britain is researched, guided and structured by the Health and Safety Executive (HSE), a government body. An EEC Directive on work with display screen equipment was completed in the early 1990s, with member states required to adapt it to become part of their own legislation. As a consequence, the Health and Safety at Work Act of 1974 incorporated legislation pertaining to the use of VDUs, and the relevant section is now referred to as The Health and Safety (Display Screen Equipment) Regulations 1992.

This legislation is intended to protect the health of employees within the working environment, and employers, employees and manufacturers all have some responsibility in conforming to the law.

Employers are required to

♦ Perform an analysis of workstations in order to evaluate the safety and health conditions to which they give rise;

♦ Provide training to employees in the use of workstation components;

♦ Ensure employees take regular breaks or changes in activity;

♦ Provide regular eye tests for workstation users and pay for glasses.

Employees have a responsibility to

♦ Use workstations and equipment correctly, in accordance with training provided by employers;

♦ Bring problems to the attention of their employer immediately and co-operate in the correction of these problems.

Manufacturers are required to ensure that their products comply with the Directive. For example, screens must tilt and swivel, keyboards must be separate and moveable. Notebook PCs are not suitable for entering large amounts of data.

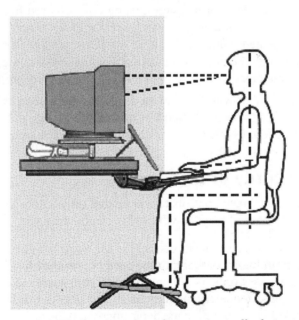

Figure 7.3: Workstations must be ergonomically designed

The ergonomic environment

Ergonomics refers to the design and functionality of the environment, and encompasses the entire range of environmental factors. Employers must give consideration to

♦ **Lighting**. The office should be well lit. Computers should neither face windows nor back onto a window so that the users have to sit with the sun in their eyes. Adjustable blinds should be provided.

♦ **Furniture**. Chairs should be of adjustable height, with a backrest which tilts to support the user at work and at rest, and should swivel on a five-point base. It should be at the correct height relative to a keyboard on the desk.

♦ **Work space**. The combination of chair, desk, computer, accessories (such as document holders, mouse and mouse mats, paper trays and so on), lighting, heating and ventilation all contribute to the worker's overall well-being.

♦ **Noise**. Noisy printers, for example, should be given covers to reduce the noise or positioned in a different room.

♦ **Hardware**. The screen must tilt and swivel and be flicker-free, the keyboard must be separately attached.

♦ **Software**. Software is often overlooked in the quest for ergonomic perfection. The EEC Directive made a clear statement about the characteristics of acceptable software, requiring employers to analyse the tasks which their employers performed and to provide software which makes the tasks easier. It is also expected to be easy to use and adaptable to the user's experience.

Software can be hazardous to your health

Bad software can be extremely stressful to use. Software that slows you down by crashing frequently, giving incomprehensible error messages, using non-standard function keys and displaying badly structured menus, for example, can leave a user longing to throw the computer from the nearest window. Repeated failure with a new software package very quickly becomes frustrating, boring and depressing. Feelings of inadequacy and alienation mean that people may begin to dread their daily encounters with the computer and productivity suffers.

Human-computer interaction is a growing field of study within computing and seeks to understand, among other things, what makes software difficult or unpleasant to use, and how it can be improved. The principles of good, usable software design are based on extensive research.

7.5   Safety and security of data

Computer systems must have adequate controls to ensure that only authorised personnel have access to data. There are a number of ways in which this can be achieved:

Passwords

Most networks require a user to log on with their password before they can gain access to the computer system. Additional passwords may be required to gain access to certain programs and data. For example in an organisation everyone may be able to access word processing programs and files, but only people working in the Finance department may be able to access the accounting system. It is clearly important that these passwords are not divulged to other people and it is recommended that passwords are frequently changed. In fact many systems are set up to automatically prompt you after a set number of days to change your password.

Communications controls

These controls ensure that only authorised people can connect to a computer from an external link. Some organisations have dial-back systems: when someone attempts to log on to the remote computer, they are positively identified and the computer disconnects them and immediately dials them back to ensure they are an authorised user.

Virus checks

Viruses are generally developed with a definite intention to cause damage to computer files or, at the very least, cause inconvenience and annoyance to computer users. The first virus appeared at the University of Delaware in 1987, and since then the number of viruses has escalated to over 9000 different variations in 1997 and tens of thousands today. The virus usually occupies the first few instructions of a particular program on an 'infected' disk and relies on a user choosing to execute that program. When an infected program is executed, the virus is the first series of instructions to be performed. In most cases the virus's first action is to copy itself from the diskette onto the PC and 'hide' within obscure files, the operating system code or within unused disk blocks which are then marked as being 'bad' and unavailable for reuse. The virus can then proceed to perform any of a number tasks ranging from the irritating to the catastrophic such as reformatting the hard disk.

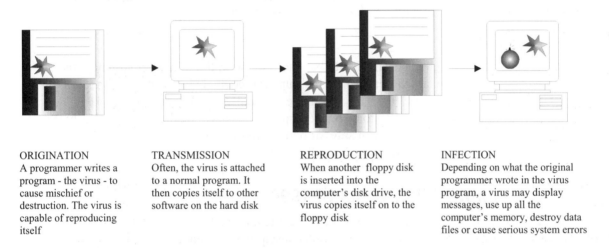

ORIGINATION
A programmer writes a program - the virus - to cause mischief or destruction. The virus is capable of reproducing itself

TRANSMISSION
Often, the virus is attached to a normal program. It then copies itself to other software on the hard disk

REPRODUCTION
When another floppy disk is inserted into the computer's disk drive, the virus copies itself on to the floppy disk

INFECTION
Depending on what the original programmer wrote in the virus program, a virus may display messages, use up all the computer's memory, destroy data files or cause serious system errors

Figure 7.4: How a virus works

Some viruses lie dormant, waiting to be triggered by a particular event or date – the 'Friday 13th' virus being a well-known one. The virus then infects other diskettes, perhaps by modifying operating system programs responsible for copying programs. From there, the next PC to use the diskette will be infected.

Virus checkers need to be installed on all computer systems so that they automatically check for any infected data when the computer is started up. Manual checkers can also be used to check for viruses on floppy disks

Saving work

It is important to save your work regularly to avoid loss. Some programs also perform automatic saves at regular intervals that you can preset. If the computer crashes, the program will recover the document from the last save it performed before the PC was restarted. This is called **Autorecovery**.

Chapter 2 gives advice on organising your files and folders so that you can easily retrieve your work. In some programs, such as Microsoft Word, you can keep a record of changes made to a document by automatically saving a different **version** of it every time the document is closed. This saves disk space because Word only saves the differences between versions, not an entire copy of each version. After you've saved several versions of a document you can go back and open, review, print or delete previous versions (but you can't edit it).

To save multiple versions of a Word document:

- With the Word document open, select **File**, **Versions**.

- Select the **Automatically save a version on close** check box.
- Click **Close**.

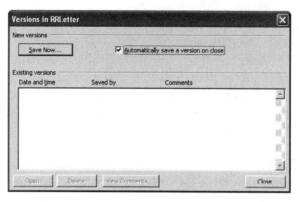

Figure 7.5: Automatically saving versions

Back-up systems

Routine back-ups of the computer system should be made so that in the case of emergency, the system can be recreated to the last full back-up. Back-ups can be made to a variety of media – magnetic tape, CD-ROM, Zip drive etc. They are made on a daily, weekly or monthly basis depending on the importance of the data to be backed up. The back-up media must be clearly labelled and should be stored in a fire-proof safe, or better still on a different site, so that should a disaster or emergency occur, the back-up media will be safe.

7.6   The Computer Misuse Act of 1990

In the early 1980s in the UK, hacking was not illegal. Some universities stipulated that hacking, especially where damage was done to data files, was a disciplinary offence, but there was no legislative framework within which a criminal prosecution could be brought. This situation was rectified by the Computer Misuse Act of 1990 which defined three specific criminal offences to deal with the problems of hacking, viruses and other nuisances. The offences are:

♦ unauthorised access to computer programs or data;

♦ unauthorised access with a further criminal intent;

♦ unauthorised modification of computer material (i.e. programs or data).

To date there have been relatively few prosecutions under this law – probably because most organisations are reluctant to admit that their system security procedures have been breached, which might lead to a loss of confidence on the part of their clients.

7.7   Principles of Data Protection

The Data Protection Act 1998 came into force on 1 March 2000. It sets rules for processing personal information and applies to paper records as well as those held on computers. It strengthens and extends the rules about data protection laid down in the Data Protection Act 1984, which it now replaces.

The rules

Anyone processing personal data must comply with the eight enforceable principles of good practice. They say that data must be:

♦   fairly and lawfully processed;

♦   processed for limited purposes;

♦   adequate, relevant and not excessive;

♦   accurate;

♦   not kept longer than necessary;

♦   processed in accordance with the data subject's rights;

♦   secure;

♦   not transferred to countries without adequate protection.

Personal data covers both facts and opinions about a living person. It also includes information regarding the intentions of the data controller towards the individual, although in some limited circumstances exemptions will apply. For more information on Data Protection visit the following web site: www.informationcommissioner.gov.uk

7.8 Sample questions

1. Which of these is NOT a principle of the Data Protection Act?

    A   Data should be accurate

    B   Data should not be kept longer than necessary

    C   Data should be secure

    D   Data should be interesting

2. What does RSI stand for?

    A   Repetitive Strain Injury

    B   Repetitive Single Injury

    C   Recurring Strained Item

    D   Returning Sight Impairment

3. A company has a major fire and the computers are damaged beyond repair. They have lost all their data. What precaution should they have taken?

    A   Allocated everyone passwords

    B   Labelled all the computers

    C   Kept backup copies of files next to the computer

    D   Kept backup copies on a different site

4. If software is copyright

    A   You can make two copies to give to friends

    B   You must not make unauthorised copies

    C   You can make as many copies as you like

    D   It does not work correctly

5. Ergonomics refers to

    A   The design and functionality of the environment

    B   A stress-related illness

    C   A spreadsheet package

    D   A type of software licence

6. What is Autorecovery?

    A   A hardware maintenance agreement

    B   Automatic recovery of a file

    C   Corrupt data

    D   A backup tape

Part 2

Information Technology

Level **3**

Chapter 8 – More on Spreadsheets

Objectives

- ❏ To import data files
- ❏ To use absolute and relative cell references
- ❏ To use a lookup table
- ❏ To sort data in a spreadsheet
- ❏ To link two worksheets
- ❏ To use advanced functions such as If.. Then.. Else
- ❏ To use a spreadsheet to do "What if?" type calculations
- ❏ To print the formulae in a spreadsheet
- ❏ To print a worksheet with a header and footer
- ❏ To protect the formulae in a worksheet so that they cannot be accidentally overwritten

8.1 Preparing for the Level 3 test

In the external test you will be required to create a specified spreadsheet structure and to import data files provided by QCA. You may be asked to edit the spreadsheet, insert formulae and functions and draw charts based on the spreadsheet data. Make sure you are familiar with the techniques covered in Chapter 4 before tackling this chapter – these chapters cover most of the skills required for the spreadsheet element of the test.

> **Sample task: To create a spreadsheet of student grades**

8.2 Determining the user requirements

Before starting work on a project for your portfolio you must find out exactly what the user requires, and plan how you are going to satisfy these requirements – 'solve the problem'. In this sample project the following facts have been explained by the teacher who wants to use the spreadsheet:

- ♦ The maximum mark varies for different exams. For this particular exam it is 78.
- ♦ Each student's mark is to be converted to a percentage.
- ♦ The grade boundaries also vary for different exams. The range of marks for each grade are known, and each student's grade should be shown alongside their percentage mark.
- ♦ The spreadsheet needs to be constructed in such a way that it can be used for other classes sitting other exams. New names, marks and grade boundaries will need to be entered but any formulae should not need to be recalculated.
- ♦ It would be useful to include the name (including pathname) of the workbook somewhere on the printout so that in a year's time the teacher will know where on the hard drive to find it.

You should discuss your progress with the user, showing them drafts of your work and seeking feedback on content, layout, format and style.

8.3 Finding the information and planning the spreadsheet

Once you have determined the user requirements you need to find the data to be used in the spreadsheet. For some spreadsheet tasks for your portfolio you may need to find statistics on the Internet (for example, share prices, exchange rates, temperatures, prices etc.). If you are not using IT to carry out any information seeking then you must carry out another activity covering a different purpose that does use IT to search for information. Record your sources on an Information Seeking record sheet (a sample is provided at www.payne-gallway.co.uk/ksit.) in your portfolio.

The next step is to spend some time with a pencil and paper planning how you are going to tackle the problem. For example:

♦ How many worksheets will you use?

♦ How will you lay them out?

♦ What formulae will you need?

Keep these notes attached to a Planning record sheet in your portfolio.

In this sample task you are given the data in the form of a comma delimited text file to be imported. (You will be given data in a similar format in the external test.) The text file is called **Grades data.txt** and can be downloaded from www.payne-gallway.co.uk/ksit. Save it in a new folder called **Grades**.

8.4 Importing the data file

• Load Excel and open a new worksheet.

• Select **Data**, **Import External Data**, **Import Data**.

• In the Select Data Source dialogue box navigate to the correct file **Grades data.txt** (make sure **Files of type** is set to **Text Files**).

• Click on the file and then click **Open**.

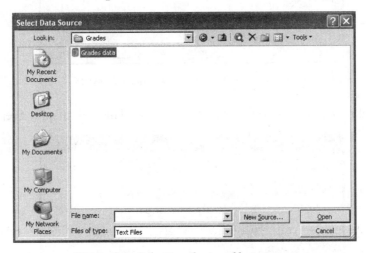

Figure 8.1: Selecting the text file to import

Step 1 of the Text Import Wizard will be displayed.

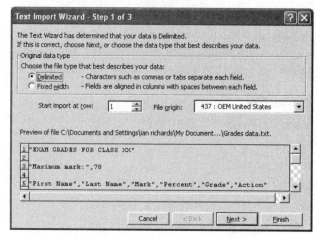

Figure 8.2: Choosing the data type

- Choose the options shown above and click **Next**. This will display Step 2 of the wizard.

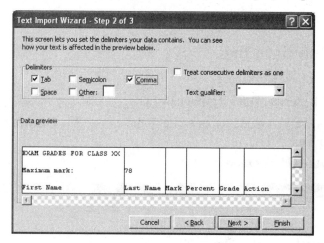

Figure 8.3: Setting the text delimiters

- Select Comma delimiters as shown above and click **Next**. This will display Step 3 of the wizard.

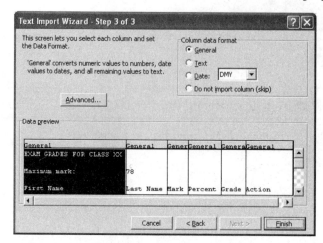

Figure 8.4: Selecting the data format

- Select **General** format (you will be asked to format the data later) and click **Finish**.
- In the final dialogue box select to put the data into an **Existing worksheet** and click **OK**.

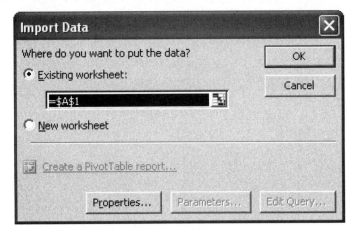

Figure 8.5

You should now see the imported data in your worksheet.

- Save the file as **ClassXX.xls** in your **Grades** folder
- Format the entries as shown in Figure 8.6, changing the font size of the heading in cell A1, making headings bold and right-justifying headings in columns C to F.

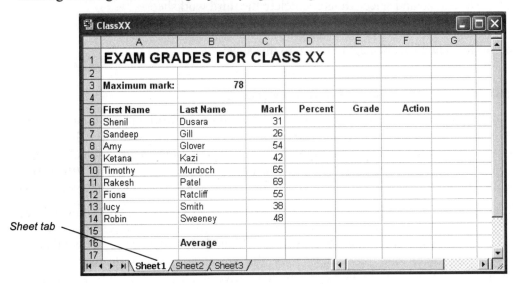

Figure 8.6: Formatting the worksheet

- Insert a formula into cell C16 to calculate the average student mark. Format this cell to 1 decimal place.

8.5 Naming and displaying worksheets

It is useful to name each worksheet rather than having them called **Sheet1**, **Sheet2** etc.

- Right-click the Sheet tab for **Sheet1** and select **Rename**.
- Type the name *Marks* and press **Enter**.

On **Sheet2** we will enter the Grade boundaries.

- Right-click the Sheet tab for **Sheet2** and select **Rename**.
- Type the name *Grade Boundaries* and press **Enter**.
- In this worksheet, type the heading and the grade boundaries as shown in Figure 8.7.

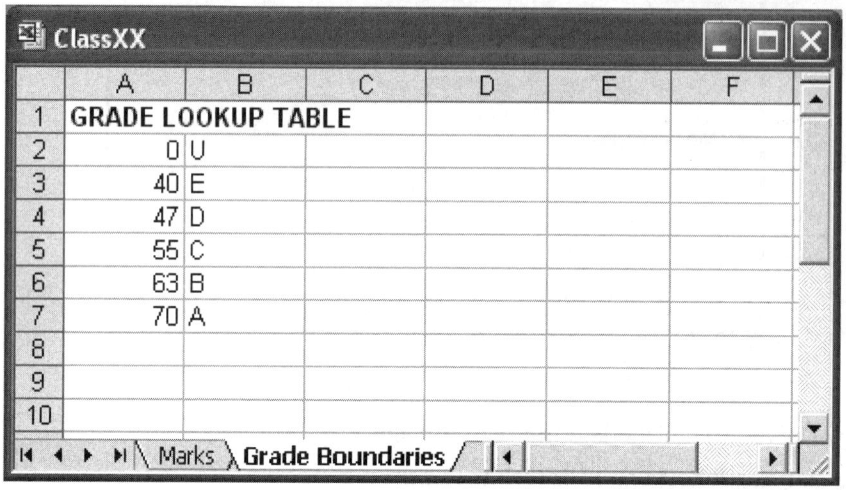

	A	B	C	D	E	F
1	GRADE LOOKUP TABLE					
2	0	U				
3	40	E				
4	47	D				
5	55	C				
6	63	B				
7	70	A				
8						
9						
10						

Figure 8.7: The Grade Boundary table

- Right-click the **Sheet3** tab and select **Delete** to delete the third worksheet.
- Save the workbook as **ClassXX**.
- Click the tab for the **Marks** worksheet to return to this sheet.

8.6 Absolute and relative cell references

The next thing to be done is to work out each mark as a percentage. To work out 31 as a percentage of 78, we need the formula (31/78)*100. Using cell references, we would need to enter the formula **=(C6/B3)*100** in cell D6. (See Figure 8.6.) However, if we copy this formula down the column, the formula in cell D7 will appear as **=(C7/B4)*100** which is not correct – it should be **=(C7/B3)*100**. In other words, although we want the marks from C7, C8, C9 etc. to be used as we move down the column, the maximum mark is always in B3.

In the formula **=(C6/B3)*100**, C6 is a **relative** reference and B3 is an **absolute** reference. The dollar sign ($) is used in front of the column letter or the row number, or both, to tell Excel that either or both of the row and column references is to be absolute and unvarying. (In some circumstances you may, for example, want the row to be relative and the column to be absolute. In this example you want both the row and column reference to be absolute.)

- In cell D6, type the formula *=C6/B3*100* and press **Enter**. (Note that you do not need the brackets in the formula although you may feel they add to the clarity.)
- Drag the handle in the bottom right-hand corner down to D14 to copy the formula to the other cells in the column.
- Click the column header D and from the menu select **Format, Cells**.
- Select the **Number** tab and change the display to **0** decimal places.

Your spreadsheet should now look like Figure 8.8. Note the formula in D14, which is visible in the Formula bar.

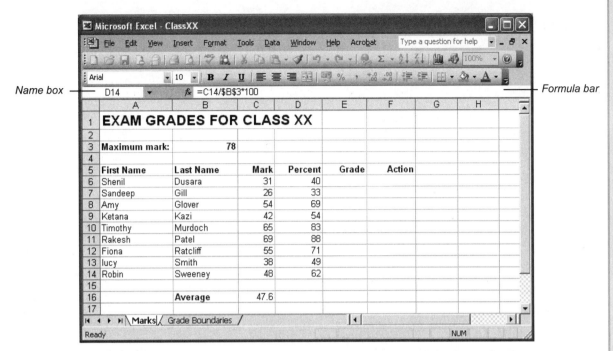

Figure 8.8: Working out percentages using a mixture of relative and absolute cell references

8.7 Naming cells

Naming cells or cell ranges can make your formulae easier to understand. We will name cell B3 **MaxMark**, and use this name in the formula for percentage instead of using the absolute reference B3. When you use a cell name in a formula, it is assumed by Excel to be an absolute reference.

- Delete the contents of D6 to D14 by selecting the cells and pressing the **Delete** key.
- Select cell B3 containing the maximum mark.
- In the Name box type the name *MaxMark* and press **Enter**.
- In cell D6 enter the formula *=C6/MaxMark*100* and press **Enter**.
- Copy this formula down to cell D14. You will get the same results as previously.

8.8 Using a lookup table

Next, we will use a function to look up the grade for each student from the table held on the **Grade Boundaries** worksheet (see Figure 8.7). First of all we will name the lookup table.

- Click the **Grade Boundaries** sheet tab to move to the worksheet.
- Select any cell inside the table and press **Ctrl-Shift-*** to select the entire table. Click in the Name box and name the table *Grade_Lookup*. Remember to press **Enter**.

Naming a Lookup table has several benefits – it makes the Lookup formula easier to read, it simplifies referring to the table as an absolute reference, it allows you to easily move the table to a different location and it eliminates the need to change the formulae if you change the size of the lookup table.

Excel has a useful function called **VLOOKUP** which enables you to look up values from a table. The table we are using is a little more complicated than some because we are looking up a *range* of values rather than a specific value. Excel looks first at the value in the first row and asks "Is the percentage grade greater than or equal 0?" If it is, it moves down a row and asks "Is the percentage grade greater than or equal to 40?" If it is not (suppose it is 39), then Excel backs up a row and assigns the grade U.

In other words, according to the table shown in Figure 8.7:

$$
\begin{array}{rcl}
0-39 & = & U \\
40-46 & = & E \\
47-54 & = & D \\
55-62 & = & C \\
63-69 & = & B \\
70-100 & = & A
\end{array}
$$

OK, let's do it!

* Move to the **Marks** worksheet.

* Click in cell E6, and click the **Insert Function** button.

* In the **Insert Function** dialogue box, select **Lookup & Reference** in the Function Category and in the Function Name list select **VLOOKUP**. Click **OK**.

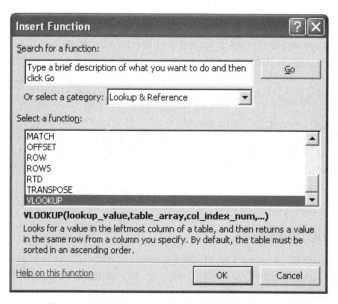

Figure 8.9: Selecting the VLOOKUP function

The VLOOKUP dialogue box appears as shown in Figure 8.10. It has three required arguments and one optional argument.

Read the explanatory text in the dialogue box, and note particularly that the table must be sorted in ascending order. VLOOKUP will not work on an unsorted table.

* Drag the dialogue box out of the way if it is obscuring your figures.

* In the **Lookup_value** box, enter *D6*, the value that you want to look up.

* In the **Table-array** box, type *Grade_Lookup*.

* In the **Col_index_num** box type *2*, because it is the second column of the lookup table that contains the grades.

- Leave the fourth argument blank, and click **OK**.

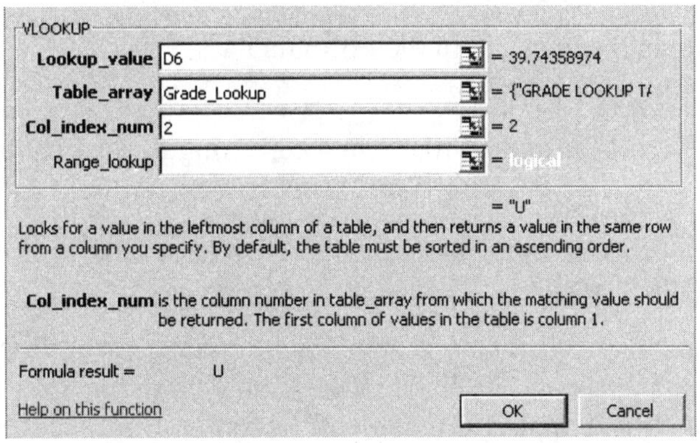

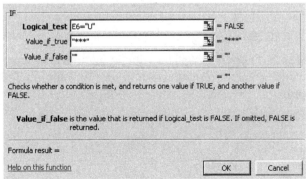

Figure 8.10: Entering the arguments for VLOOKUP

Excel assigns a grade U to the first student, Shenil Dusara. But we were expecting it to be a grade E! What is wrong?

The answer is that when we formatted the Percent column, Excel shows the figure to the nearest whole number but it still holds the value 39.7435974, which is less than 40 and so gets a grade U. To cure this problem we need to round the percentage to the nearest whole number. Then the value held by Excel will be the same value as it displays.

To do this we can use another function, **ROUND**.

- Click in cell D6 and Edit the formula in the formula bar so that it reads
  =ROUND(C6/MaxMark*100, 0). This rounds the result to 0 decimal places.

The grade in cell E6 should change to E.

- Copy the formula down to D14.

- Copy the formula in cell E6 down the rest of the column.

You should test the formula carefully. The most likely places for errors to occur are on the boundaries between grades. Keep changing the marks until you are satisfied that your spreadsheet gives correct answers whatever the mark is.

8.9   Using an If.. Then.. Else function

In the Action column, we will put three asterisks (***) against any student who has a Grade U.

- Click in cell F6 and press the **Insert Function** button.

- Select the **Logical** category and the **IF** function from the list. Fill in the dialogue box as shown in Figure 8.11.

Figure 8.11: The IF function

- Copy the formula down the column. Only the students with a Grade U should have an asterisk in column F.

- Have a look at the formula that appears in the Formula bar.

=IF(E7="U","***","")

- Note that you can write an **IF** formula directly in a cell using this format instead of using the Function Wizard. The format is **IF(condition, Value if true, Value if false)**

8.10 Sorting a worksheet

You can sort the records in a worksheet very easily using the **Sort Ascending** or the **Sort Descending** button. Suppose you want to sort the records in descending order of mark, i.e. the student with the highest mark will appear at the top of the list.

- Click anywhere in column C within the data area.

- Click the **Sort Descending** button on the Standard toolbar.

If you want to perform a more complex sort, for example sorting in ascending order of grade and within that, in ascending order by name, you can do so using a menu option.

- Make sure that the current cell is somewhere in the data area.

- From the menu select **Data, Sort**.

A dialogue box appears and the data area is highlighted.

- Fill in the dialogue box as shown in Figure 8.12.

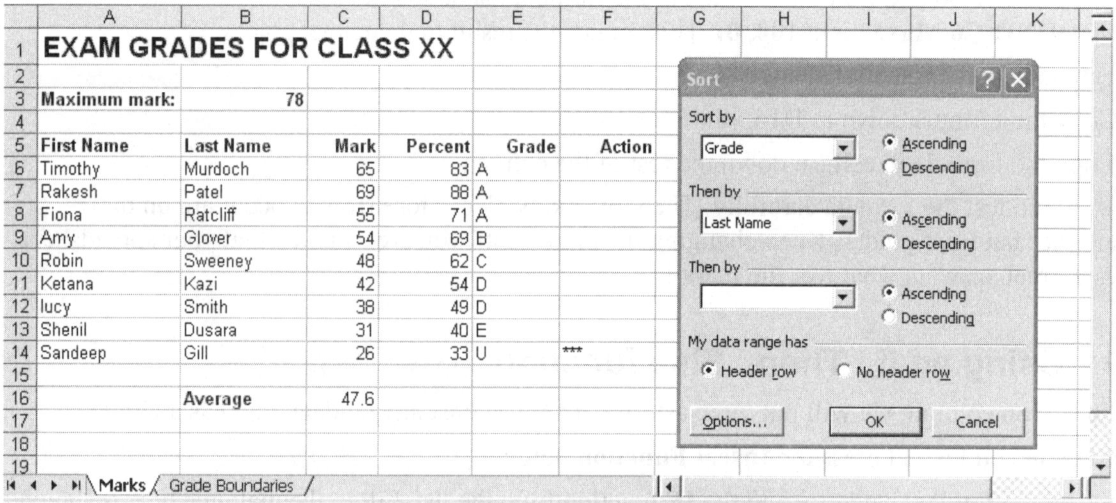

Figure 8.12: Sorting on more than one field

8.11 Headers and footers

You can add a header and footer to your worksheet which will appear when it is printed or displayed in Print Preview mode. The information in a header or footer includes such things as the file name, sheet name, your name, page number, date printed etc.

- From the main menu select **View, Header and Footer…** A dialogue box appears.

- Fill in the dialogue box as shown in Figure 8.13.

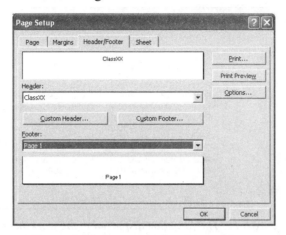

Figure 8.13: Inserting a header and footer

- If you want to insert additional information such as your own name and the date, click on **Custom Header...** or **Custom Footer...** and another dialogue box appears where you can enter anything you wish. Click **OK** when you are done.

- Click the **Print Preview** button to see how your worksheet looks with the header and footer.

Sometimes (perhaps in the external test) you only want to print certain cells. You can do this by setting the **print area**.

- In the spreadsheet highlight the cells you want to print.

- Select **File**, **Print area**, **Set Print area**.

A dotted line will appear around the cells to be printed. You can check it is correct in Print Preview and then print as usual.

8.12 Printing the spreadsheet formulae

For the purposes of documentation or providing evidence of the formulae you have used, you may need to print out the spreadsheet formulae.

- Select **Tools, Options** and click the **View** tab. Check the **Formulas** box as shown below, and click **OK**.

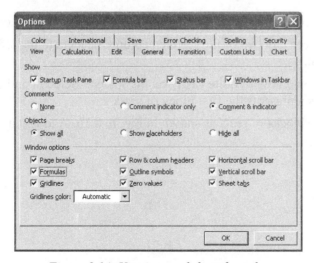

Figure 8.14: Viewing worksheet formulae

After some adjustment of the column widths, the worksheet appears as shown in Figure 8.15.

	A	B	C	D	E	F
1	**EXAM G**					
2						
3	Maximum m	78				
4						
5	**First Name**	**Last Name**	**Mark**	**Percent**	**Grade**	**Action**
6	Timothy	Murdoch	65	=ROUND(C6/MaxMark*100,0)	=VLOOKUP(D6,Grade_Lookup,2)	=IF(E6="U","****","")
7	Rakesh	Patel	69	=ROUND(C7/MaxMark*100,0)	=VLOOKUP(D7,Grade_Lookup,2)	=IF(E7="U","****","")
8	Fiona	Ratcliff	55	=ROUND(C8/MaxMark*100,0)	=VLOOKUP(D8,Grade_Lookup,2)	=IF(E8="U","****","")
9	Amy	Glover	54	=ROUND(C9/MaxMark*100,0)	=VLOOKUP(D9,Grade_Lookup,2)	=IF(E9="U","****","")
10	Robin	Sweeney	48	=ROUND(C10/MaxMark*100,0)	=VLOOKUP(D10,Grade_Lookup,2)	=IF(E10="U","****","")
11	Ketana	Kazi	42	=ROUND(C11/MaxMark*100,0)	=VLOOKUP(D11,Grade_Lookup,2)	=IF(E11="U","****","")
12	lucy	Smith	38	=ROUND(C12/MaxMark*100,0)	=VLOOKUP(D12,Grade_Lookup,2)	=IF(E12="U","****","")
13	Shenil	Dusara	31	=ROUND(C13/MaxMark*100,0)	=VLOOKUP(D13,Grade_Lookup,2)	=IF(E13="U","****","")
14	Sandeep	Gill	26	=ROUND(C14/MaxMark*100,0)	=VLOOKUP(D14,Grade_Lookup,2)	=IF(E14="U","****","")
15						
16		**Average**	=AVERAGE(C6:C14)			
17						

Figure 8.15: The formulae displayed in the worksheet

You can print this out for portfolio evidence. To return to the normal view, select **Tools, Options** again and uncheck **Formulas** in the **View Options** dialogue box (Figure 8.14).

- That ends this exercise, so save and close your worksheet.

Sample task: Creating a seating plan and budget for a gig

In this exercise you will use Excel to create a seating plan for some sort of theatrical event or gig, on which you can show which seats have been booked. On a second, linked worksheet you will work out how much money you will make on the sale of these tickets. This second worksheet can also be used to help plan how much you should charge for tickets so that the event does not lose money.

8.13 Creating a seating plan for a gig

- Open a new workbook.
- To create the seating plan, start in cell C4 and drag down to cell AF8.
- Select **Format, Cells** and click the **Border** tab. Click the **Outline** and **Inside** buttons and click **OK**.
- Now drag across the column headers of columns A to AF to select these columns.
- Drag the border between any two of the selected column headers to the left to make each cell approximately square.

- The bordered area should now fit quite easily on the screen. Select it and use the **Fill** tool to colour it yellow. This represents the first block of seats.
- Now create two more blocks of seats as shown in Figure 8.16. Add text as shown.

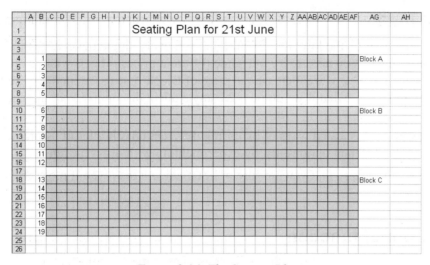

Figure 8.16: The Seating Plan

- Right-click the **Sheet1** tab and select **Rename**. Type the name *Seating Plan* and press **Enter**.

- Save your workbook, naming it **Gig**.

8.14 Creating a budget spreadsheet

Now we will move to **Sheet2** and work out how much to charge for tickets. Suppose you have the following facts:

- The total cost of the gig will be about £4,000.

- There are 150 seats in Block A, 210 seats in each of Blocks B and C. (Block C is at the front and you can charge more for these seats.)

- You are to have two different types of ticket: Full-price and Student tickets, which will be somewhat cheaper.

- You must try not to make a loss on the event, which you hope is going to be a sell-out.

We're ready to start!

- Right-click the **Sheet2** tab and rename it *Ticket Sales*. Press **Enter**.

- Enter the headings and figures as shown in Figure 8.17. Note that cell B14 has a formula in it, adding up the total possible income from each block of seats if they are all sold at full price.

- Work out what the formula in cell C14 should be and enter it. If you get it right the figure 2025 as shown will appear!

B14	▼	ƒx	=150*B8+210*B9+210*B10		
	A	B	C	D	E
1					
2					
3					
4	Total number of seats		570		
5					
6		Price per seat			
7		Full Price	Student		
8	Block A	£6.00	£3.00		
9	Block B	£7.00	£3.50		
10	Block C	£8.00	£4.00		
11					
12					
13		Full Price	Student		
14	Max. possible income:	£4,050.00	£2,025.00		
15					

Figure 8.17: Working out ticket prices

- Format the worksheet so that it appears as in Figure 8.17.

8.15 What if...?

The seat prices are rather on the low side. Even if you sell every single ticket at the full price, you will only just break even. You need to try out some different prices. This is what is meant by doing "What if?" calculations; what if we increase the price of Block A seats, or increase the full price seat prices for all blocks, or what if we do not give any student discounts? Will this have an adverse effect on ticket sales?

Excel has some very sophisticated ways of exploring different possibilities or 'scenarios'. However, you can easily try out different options just by experimenting with different figures.

* Change the ticket prices so that you are sure of not making a loss even if most of the ticket sales are student sales.

8.16 The CountIf function

Now we are going to link the two worksheets together. This simply means that we will use a formula in the **Ticket Sales** sheet that references one or more cells in the **Seating Plan** sheet.

On the seating plan, every time a seat is sold at the Student price we will type **S** in the cell. Every time a seat is sold at the full price, we will type **F** in the cell. In the **Ticket Sales** sheet, we need to count up the number of S's and F's in each block and enter these numbers. We can use formulae to calculate the total income from ticket sales.

Excel has a useful function called COUNTIF which will do the trick here. Before entering the formulae, however, we will name the blocks of seats so that they will be easier to refer to.

* In the Seating Plan sheet, select the whole of Block A.
* From the menu select **Insert, Name, Define**.
* Enter the name *BlockA* and click **OK**.
* Name Block B and Block C in a similar way. (See Figure 8.18.)

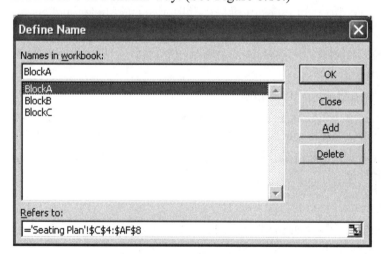

Figure 8.18: Naming the blocks of seats

Now we're ready to enter the headings and formulae to work out ticket income.

* Enter the headings in the **Ticket Sales** worksheet as shown in Figure 8.19. Keep them in the same row and columns as shown or your formulae will be different.

		Number of seats sold		
16				
17		**Number of seats sold**		
18		**Full Price**	**Student**	**Empty**
19	**Block A**			
20	**Block B**			
21	**Block C**			
22				
23		**Income from ticket sales**		
24		**Full Price**	**Student**	
25	**Block A**			
26	**Block B**			
27	**Block C**			
28				
29	Total			
30				

Figure 8.19: Preparing to calculate income from ticket sales

- Click cell B19 to make it the active cell.
- Click the **Insert Function** button.
- In the dialogue box, select the **Statistical** category and the **COUNTIF** function from the list.
- Enter the parameters as shown in Figure 8.20, and click **OK**.

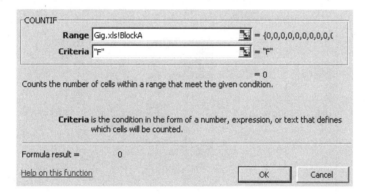

Figure 8.20: Counting the number of cells in Block A that contain "F"

This counts the number of cells in Block A that contain F. Test out the formula by typing *F* in several seats in Block A.

- Notice that the formula in the cell is **=COUNTIF(Gig.xls!BlockA,"F")**. You can enter a similar formula in cell C19, replacing **"F"** with **"S"**.
- In cell D19, you want to enter the number of empty seats. The formula is **=COUNTIF(Gig.xls!BlockA,"")**.
- Enter similar formulae in cells B20 to D21.
- Now you can work out the income from ticket sales. In cell B25, enter the formula *=B8*B19*.
- Copy this formula to cells B26 and B27, and to cells C25 to C27.
- In cell B29, enter a formula to sum cells B25 to B27.
- Copy this formula to cell C29.
- In cell D29, enter a formula to find the total ticket sales.
- Enter a few more S's and F's in your seating plan and test your worksheet. It should look something like Figure 8.21 though you may have chosen different seat prices and a different number of seats sold in each block.

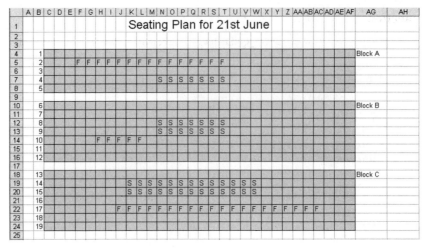

Figure 8.21: Seat bookings

The Ticket Income worksheet should now reflect these bookings and look like Figure 8.22:

	A	B	C	D	E	F
1						
2						
3						
4	Total number of seats		570			
5						
6		Price per seat				
7		Full Price	Student			
8	Block A	£6.00	£3.00			
9	Block B	£7.00	£3.50			
10	Block C	£8.00	£4.00			
11						
12						
13		Full Price	Student			
14	Max. possible income:	£4,050.00	£2,025.00			
15						
16						
17		Number of seats sold				
18		Full Price	Student	Empty		
19	Block A	15	7	128		
20	Block B	5	14	191		
21	Block C	20	26	164		
22						
23		Income from ticket sales				
24		Full Price	Student			
25	Block A	£90.00	£21.00			
26	Block B	£35.00	£49.00			
27	Block C	£160.00	£104.00			
28						
29	Total	£285.00	£174.00	£459.00		
30						

Figure 8.22: The Ticket Income worksheet

8.17 Protecting a worksheet

When you have got the worksheet to this point and tested the formulae thoroughly, it would be a good idea to go back to the user and make sure that it is exactly what they want. Document this process of consultation and make a note of any changes that you have been asked to make.

When you and the user are satisfied that no more changes are needed, you can protect the worksheet so that the user cannot accidentally wipe out or change any of the formulae you have entered.

By default, all cells will be automatically locked if you protect the worksheet. Therefore you must unlock any cells in which data entry is allowed, and then protect the worksheet. (You may not be able to do this on a college or school machine with restricted access.)

- In the **Ticket Sales** worksheet select cells B8 to C10 containing ticket prices.
- From the **Format** menu select **Cells**.

- Click the **Protection** tab and clear the **Locked Cells** box.

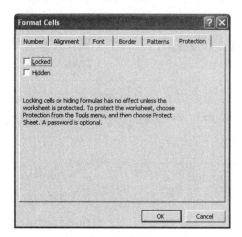

Figure 8.23: Unlocking cells for the user to enter data

You can shade the cells in which the user can enter data, and add a comment so that the user can see which cells are unprotected.

- With cells B8 to C10 still selected, press the **Fill Color** button to fill with a colour.
- Right-click the mouse button and select **Insert Comment** from the pop-up menu.
- Type the comment *Enter seat prices here* and move the comment box out of the way of the other cells.
- Right-click again and select **Show Comment** if you want the comment permanently displayed.

	Price per seat		Enter seat prices here	
	Full Price	Student		
Block A	£6.00	£3.00		
Block B	£7.00	£3.50		
Block C	£8.00	£4.00		

Figure 8.24: Entering a comment for the user

- Select **Tools, Protection, Protect Sheet**.
- There is no need to enter a password, as you are only protecting against accidental changes. Leave the password box blank and click **OK**.
- Test out your changes. You should see a message if you try to enter data in any cell except the ones that you unlocked.

That completes this exercise so save and close your worksheet.

8.18 Documenting the project

A spreadsheet application like the ones described in this chapter could form the basis of the "major task" required for the Level 3 portfolio. As soon as you decide on a project, you should start to document your planning, any research or information retrieval you have had to carry out, and your spreadsheet designs. Take regular printouts to show how your ideas have developed and annotate these printouts, perhaps to explain why you have changed layouts, formats etc. as you worked on the project. Print out the formulae in the spreadsheets and include them in your documentation.

8.19 Relating this chapter to the specification

Specification Reference (Part B)	What you have done to satisfy this
IT3.1	
Plan how to obtain and use the information required for your tasks	• Planning the spreadsheet
Make selections based on judgements of relevance and quality.	• Internet searches • Get data from user • Selecting the appropriate data to include in formulae etc.
IT3.2	
Enter and bring together information using formats that help development	• Sorting the worksheet • Formatting the worksheet
Use software features to improve the efficiency of your work	• Using a lookup table • Protecting the formulae • 'What if' predictions • Use of formulae and functions
Annotate/document your work to show that you have understood the processes followed and have taken account of the views of others	• Sharing drafts with the user to confirm requirements
IT3.3	
Develop the presentation so it is accurate, clear and presented consistently, taking account of the views of others	• Headers and footers • Naming worksheets • Naming cells • Seeking the views of the user
Present your final output effectively using a format and style that suits your purpose and audience.	• Formatting the spreadsheets • Seating plan • Testing the formulae • Checking your work

8.20 Other Key Skills signposting

Application of Number   N3.1 Plan an activity and get relevant information

                                 N3.2 Carry out multi-stage calculations using formulae

                                 N3.3 Interpret results of calculations. Present findings and justify methods.

8.21 Evidence for your portfolio

There are numerous applications of spreadsheets that you could develop to use as evidence for your portfolio. You may be able to find a suitable topic from one of your other areas of study, especially if you are doing, say, Geography or one of the Sciences. For example you may use a spreadsheet to log the height of a river at different times, or to record temperatures, rainfall, hours of sunshine, movement of planets, experimental results, etc. You can calculate averages, maxima and minima. You can plot the data on charts of different types and include the charts in a word-processed report.

If you are a Business Studies student, you could use a spreadsheet to work out a budget or a Profit and Loss report for a business. Even if you are not doing Business Studies, you can calculate a budget for a school trip, holiday, theatre production or other event. This can be used for 'What-if' calculations to explore the effect of different price options. You could use a spreadsheet to record the ticket sales and expenses of an event such as a disco, or to keep the accounts of a Club or small business.

If you are interested in Stocks and Shares, you could keep track of a real or imaginary portfolio over a period of time. You can look up prices on the Internet, which will fulfil the requirement to use IT to look up information. Perhaps you could get a group of fellow students together and organise a competition to see who can make the most money on an imaginary portfolio – you will learn a lot about the ups and downs of the Stock Market!

The table below shows the evidence that you could collect if you decide to do a spreadsheet project. Of course, it will vary slightly depending on the type of project you select.

Type of evidence	✔
A written description of the activity	
Notes on sources of data	
Planning notes (hand-drawn sketches of layout etc.)	
Notes of discussions with the user at all stages of the project	
Earlier versions of the worksheet printouts annotated with amendments to be made and why (e.g. comments from others etc.)	
Notes on formulae and functions used	
Final printouts of the worksheets	
Printouts of worksheets displaying the formulae used	
Record from your assessor of how you developed and presented the presentation	

8.22 Sample questions

1. Create a new spreadsheet using a suitable file name.
2. Set up a spreadsheet model to calculate invoice amounts for consultancy fees which are payable by customers whose details are shown below.

Customer name	Consultancy hours	Rate per hour	Fees due	VAT (17.5%)	Total due
Wings Garden Centre	10	£30.00			
Herby Health shop	2	£30.00			
Jays Restaurant	45	£30.00			
K. Hinge & Son	28	£25.00			
Pipers Cafe	6	£30.00			
Jones Builders Merchants	12	£20.00			
Technoplace Ltd	20	£20.00			
Wellings Brothers	42	£25.00			
Mike Reep Bakers	14	£25.00			

3. Enter a formula in the **Fees due** column to calculate the fees for Wings Garden Centre.
    i.e. **Consultancy hours** multiplied by **Rate per hour**
4. Copy the formula down the column to obtain fees due for all the customers.
5. Enter a formula at the bottom of the **Fees due** column to find the total for all customers.
6. Ensure the column headings (except for **Customer name**) are right-aligned.
7. Ensure that **Consultancy hours** are displayed as integer values and all columns containing currency are displayed to 2 decimal places.
8. Enter a formula to calculate the **VAT** for Wings Garden Centre and copy the formula down the column.
    i.e.   **Fees due** multiplied by 17.5%
9. Enter a formula to calculate the **Total due.**
    i.e.   **Fees due** + **VAT**
10. Add a new customer *Kingsley Buildings* who have had 5 hours consultancy at £25.00 per hour.
11. Save the spreadsheet.
12. Print the spreadsheet.
13. Print the spreadsheet displaying the formulae used.

Chapter 9 – PowerPoint Presentations

Objectives

- ❑ To learn how to structure a presentation
- ❑ To create, edit, add and delete slides for a PowerPoint presentation
- ❑ To add Clip Art, graphs, animation and sound to a presentation
- ❑ To print out slides for documentation or to give to the audience
- ❑ To learn how to deliver an effective presentation

> **Sample task: Prepare a PowerPoint presentation on "Organic Pig Farming – A Success Story"**

In this chapter you will learn how to create and deliver a presentation. We will be concentrating on the facilities of Microsoft PowerPoint and how to make the best use of them. You are unlikely to be tested on these techniques but they will be useful for your portfolio evidence for Key Skill **IT3.3: Present Information**.

9.1   Finding the information and planning the presentation

Planning your own presentation will involve using different sources such as newspapers, books, CDs and the Internet to research the chosen topic. You must record your sources on an Information Seeking record sheet like the one provided at www.payne-gallway.co.uk/ksit. In this sample task you are given the information to include in the presentation.

In designing and planning the presentation you will need to take into account how long the presentation is to be, where and how it is to be delivered, and to whom. The contents of each slide can then be planned and special effects such as sound and animation added to spice it up and keep your audience riveted. Drawing out some rough sketches of the slides by hand before you start using PowerPoint is also a good idea. Keep notes of your planning process on a Planning record sheet.

Here are a few basic tips for designing a presentation:

- ♦ Start with a title screen showing what the project is about.
- ♦ Do not put more than 4 or 5 points on each slide. People cannot absorb too much information at once.
- ♦ Keep each point short and simple. You can expand on the points shown during your presentation – the text on the slide acts as a reminder of what you want to cover.
- ♦ Use sound, animation and graphics to maintain interest, but don't overdo them!

It will help if you can discuss the presentation with a representative of the audience to get their feedback on the content, style, layout and format of your presentation.

9.2 Starting PowerPoint

- To load PowerPoint, you can either double-click the PowerPoint icon, *or*
- Click **Start**, **Programs**, then select **Microsoft PowerPoint.**

The following screen appears:

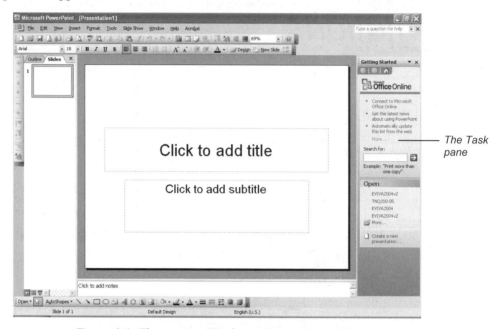

Figure 9.1: The opening Window in PowerPoint 2003

- In the Getting Started Task pane click **Create a new presentation**. The New Presentation Task pane will be displayed. Click on **From design template**.
- Now select a template. You can browse through to select a suitable one.

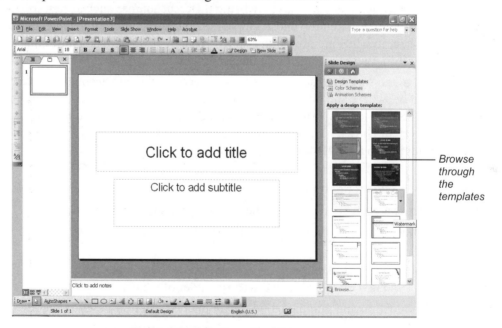

Figure 9.2: Selecting a template

- Click on the **Watermark** template.
- Click on the small black down-arrow at the top of the Task pane and select **Slide Layout**. The Slide Layout Task pane will be displayed. Click the **Title Slide** layout. This is the most suitable layout for the title page of your presentation.

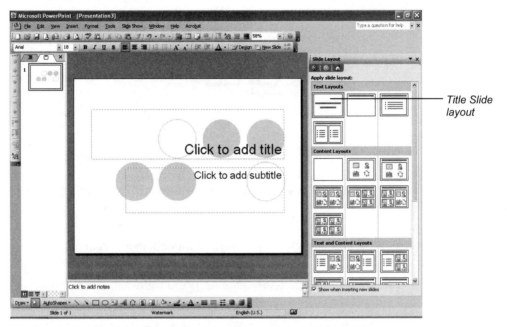

Figure 9.3: Choosing a layout for the first slide

Each slide layout has 'placeholders' in appropriate places.

- Click the **Title** placeholder and type the text *Organic Pig Farming*.
- Click where indicated and type the sub-title *A Success Story* as shown below.
- You can edit or format the text in a text box by highlighting it and then using the tools on the formatting toolbar. The text font in the sub-title below has been changed to **Tempus sans ITC**.

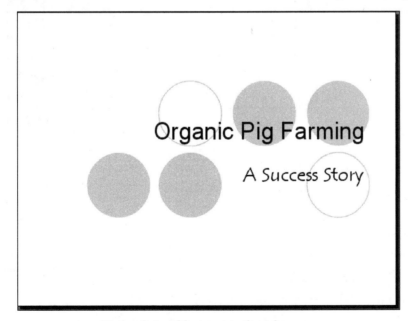

Figure 9.4: Adding text to the title screen

9.3 Changing the view

You can alternate between various views of the presentation by clicking on the icons at the bottom left of the screen.

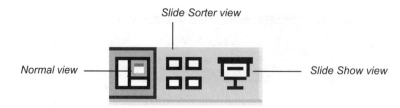

Figure 9.5: Presentation views

At the moment, **Normal View** is highlighted and the screen looks like Figure 9.6. (If it does not, click the **Normal View** icon.)

Normal View also displays allows you to display the outline on the left and the notes pane at the bottom right. You can make changes to a slide either by altering it in the slide itself or in the outline on the left.

You can browse through the other views – we will examine them again later when you have more slides to look at.

- Close the Task pane by clicking the **Close** icon in its top right-hand corner (don't confuse this with the Close Window icon).

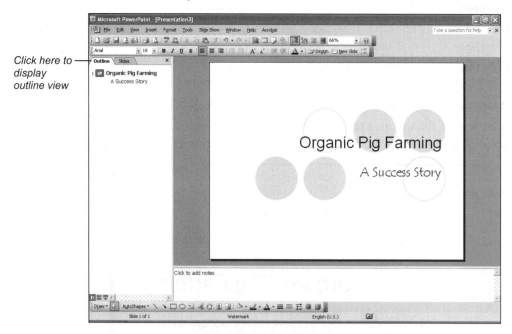

Figure 9.6: Normal view

9.4 Adding a new slide

Now you can create the second slide of the presentation.

- Click the **New Slide** icon on the Standard toolbar.

A different layout, **Title and Text**, is already selected for you which is fine.

- From the menu you can select **View, Zoom** to make the slide bigger or smaller.

- Enter the text as shown in Figure 9.7.

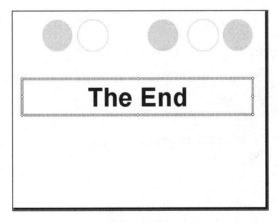

The meteoric rise in organic farming can be attributed to many factors:

- Successive food scares: BSE, E-coli, salmonella
- Concern about GM (genetically modified) products
- Fear of pesticide residues in non-organic produce
- A perception that excessive use of artificial fertilisers is harmful to the environment.

Figure 9.7: Slide 2 – A bulleted list

- You may need to reduce the default text size to fit all the text in. You can do this by highlighting the text and using the **Font Size** button on the Formatting toolbar. Alternatively, you can use the **Increase Font Size** and **Decrease Font Size** buttons to alter the size of the text to fit into a given space.

- Check the spelling in each box by clicking somewhere in the text and then clicking the **Spelling** tool on the Standard toolbar.

- Add one more slide. Make sure the slide shown in Figure 9.7 is on the screen, and then click the **New Slide** icon to insert a new slide after the current one.
- Select the **Title Only** layout, which is the second one in Figure 9.3.
- Add text *The End*. Increase the font size, bold and centre it as shown in Figure 9.8. Drag the text box to the centre of the slide.

The End

Figure 9.8

9.5 Viewing the presentation

You can view your slide show at any time by clicking the **Slide Show** icon at the bottom of the screen.

- On the left of the screen, click the **Slides** tab and then click the **Slide 1** icon.
- Click the **Slide Show** icon. Click the mouse to go to the next slide.

9.6 Saving, closing and opening your presentation

Don't forget to save your presentation every few minutes.

- Select **File, Save** from the menu bar. Save your presentation as **Pigs.ppt** or some such suitable title. You don't need to type the file extension **.ppt** which is automatically added by PowerPoint.

- You can now close your presentation if you wish by selecting **File, Close** from the menu.

- To open an existing presentation, use the **Open** section on PowerPoint's opening Task pane (as shown in Figure 9.1). Your most recently saved presentations will be listed and you can select **Pigs.ppt** from the list.

9.7 Adding a chart

On the next slide of the presentation you will add a chart.

- Click on Slide 2 at the left of the screen and it will appear in the main window.

- Click the **New Slide** icon to insert a new slide after Slide 2.

- Select the **Chart** layout from the Slide Layout Task pane as shown in Figure 9.9.

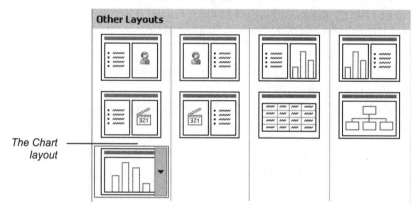

Figure 9.9: The Chart layout

Your screen should now look like Figure 9.10.

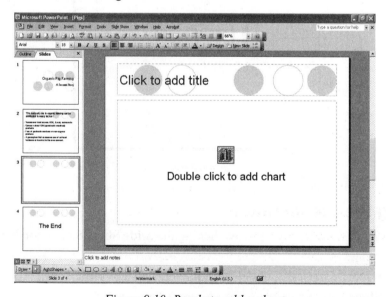

Figure 9.10: Ready to add a chart

- Type the title: *Increase in the range of organic products in a major supermarket chain:*
- Click the **Decrease Font Size** icon until the title fits neatly into its box.
- Double-click the **Chart** placeholder that PowerPoint has created on the slide.
- You will see the following chart appear:

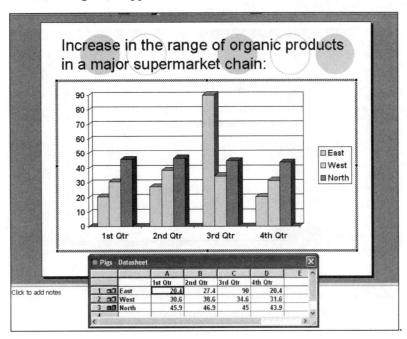

Figure 9.11: Creating a chart

To make your own chart you need to add your own information into the table.

- Click in the cell **1ˢᵗ Qtr** and type 2001. In the next two cells type 2002 and 2003.
- Right-click in column header D and select **Delete** to delete this column.
- Right-click the row headers for rows 2 and 3 and delete them.
- Highlight the entry **East** in row 1 and delete it (without deleting the entire column).
- Enter the figures as shown in Figure 9.12.

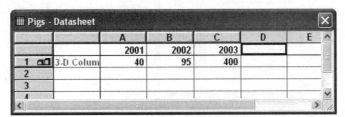

Figure 9.12: Entering the chart data

- Click the **Legend** on the right of the chart and press the **Delete** key to delete it.
- Click the **Slide Show** icon to see what your slide looks like.
- Press **Esc** to return to Normal view.
- To edit a chart, simply double-click it and the spreadsheet appears ready for you to edit. You can look at **Chart, Chart Options** on the menu bar for other features.
- Remember to save your work regularly.

9.8 Changing the Design Template or colour scheme

You may decide that your slides need a different background or colour scheme. We'll start by applying a different Design Template to all the slides.

- From the menu select **Format, Slide Design**. Select a different template from the Slide Design Task pane. The one shown in Figure 9.13 is **Capsules.pot**.

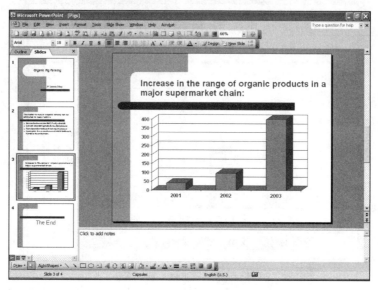

Figure 9.13: Changing the Design Template

You can also change the colour scheme without changing the Design Template.

- With any slide selected click the **Design** button on the Formatting toolbar.
- Click **Color Schemes** in the Slide Design Task pane.

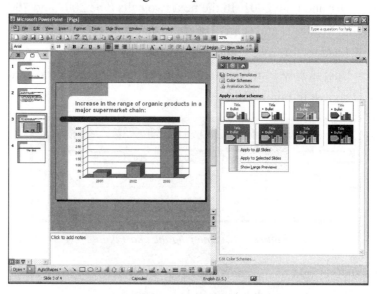

Figure 9.14: Changing the slide colour scheme

- Select a new colour scheme and click **Apply to selected slides** to change just the current slide.
- You can click the **Slide Sorter View** icon at the bottom of the screen to see all your slides so far. They will appear as shown in Figure 9.15.

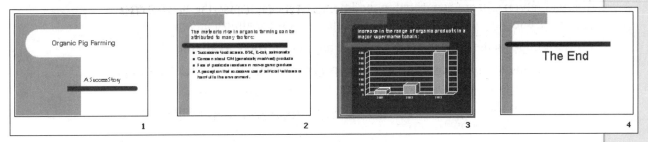

Figure 9.15: The slides in Slide Sorter view

9.9   Inserting Clip Art

On the next slide we will insert a Clip Art picture.

- Return to Normal view.
- Click the Slide 3 icon to select it and then click the New Slide icon to insert a slide after this one.
- Select the first **Title, Text and Content** layout.
- Type the text as shown in Figure 9.16.

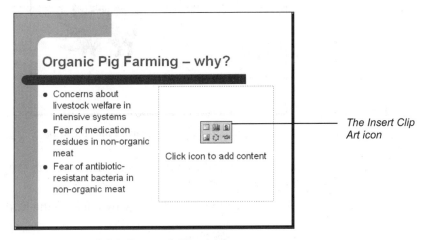

Figure 9.16: Text and Clip Art layout

- Double-click the **Insert Clip Art** icon and the Insert Clip Art dialogue box appears.

There is a limited number of clips provided with PowerPoint and you will need the Media Content CD supplied with the Microsoft Office CD to access it.

Figure 9.17: Searching for Clip Art offline

Alternatively, if you are connected to the Internet you can display the Insert Clip Art Task pane and gain access to hundreds of suitable clips for almost any presentation.

- Right-click on the arrow next to an image and select **Make available offline**.

- In the Copy to Collection window click on **My Collections** and click **OK**.

- Close the Clip Art Task pane and click the Insert Clip Art icon on your PowerPoint slide. This time you should see the new downloaded clip in the Insert Picture window.

Figure 9.18: The Clip Art Task pane

- Click the image and then click **OK**. The Clip Art will be inserted into the slide.

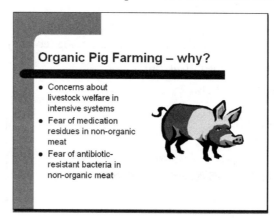

Figure 9.19: Clip Art inserted into the slide

- Note that if you click the graphic, handles will appear which you can drag to change the size of the image.

- Click the icon for Slide 1 and try out your slide show by clicking the **Slide Show** icon at the bottom of the screen.

- Save your presentation.

9.10 Inserting text boxes, sounds and animation

You need two more slides first.

- Click the icon for Slide 5 ("The End") and click the **New Slide** icon.

- Select the **Title Only** layout. Type the text *Organic Pig Farming – A success story from Poland*

- Add another new slide, this time selecting the Bulleted list layout.

- Type the title *Background – Poland has two major problems*

- Add the following text:

    ▪ *Pork prices are being undercut by a flood of imports from abroad*

- Make sure the Drawing toolbar is visible. If it is not, select **View, Toolbars** from the menu and check **Drawing**.

- Use the **Text Box** tool to add a second text box to the slide:

    "Brown coal" produced by Polish coalmines is a very polluting energy source and the mines may have to be closed down, causing substantial job losses

- Click the **Bullet** tool on the Formatting toolbar to turn it into a bullet point.
- Position the text boxes as shown in Figure 9.20. Next we will download and place a picture of a pig, the sound of pigs grunting and an animated graphic of a factory belching smoke.

Figure 9.20: Different types of object inserted into a slide

- Now click anywhere on the screen (not in a text box) and select **Insert, Picture, Clip Art** from the menu.

Search for some pictures, sounds and animations. (The factory one was found by typing **Factory** in the **Search For:** box.) If you're connected to the Internet the Microsoft web site will automatically be searched. If you want to go to the site yourself, click **Clip art on Office Online** at the bottom of the **Clip Art** task pane.

- When you insert a sound, you will see a message:

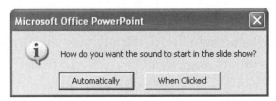

Figure 9.21: Inserting a sound into a slide

- Whichever option you choose, you can play the sound any time in Slide Show view by clicking it.
- Insert the animation.

9.11 Changing Slide Layout, moving and deleting slides

We'll add one more slide to the end of the presentation and then move it.

- Click Slide 7 and click the **New Slide** icon.

- Add a new slide, selecting the **Bulleted List** layout. Type the heading *Solution!*

Now suppose you decide that this is the wrong slide layout.

- From the menu select **Format, Slide Layout**. Select the Title Slide layout and click **OK**.
- Type the subtitle *Brown coal is fed to pigs as a dietary supplement.*

Slide 5 ("The End") is in the wrong place. It needs to be moved down.

- In Normal View, click and drag the icon for Slide 5 down to the bottom.

9.12 Changing the order of and demoting bullet points

- Insert one more new slide before the last slide. Select the **Bulleted List** layout.
- Type the title *Benefits*.
- Type bullet points as shown below.

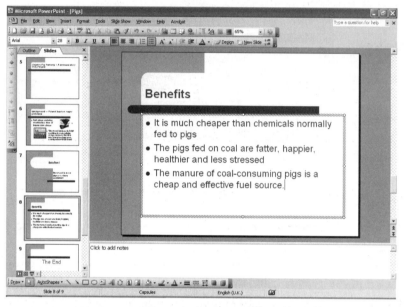

Figure 9.22: Slide 8

- Highlight and drag the second bullet point to the top of the list.
- Edit the second bullet point so that it just says *It is much cheaper*. Press **Enter**.
- Add two more bullet points as follows:
  - *Less costly than chemicals normally fed to pigs*
  - *Does not have to be administered by a vet*
- Highlight these two bullet points and click the **Demote** button on the Outlining toolbar. If this toolbar is not displayed select **View**, **Toolbars**, **Outlining** from the main menu.

The slide should now appear as follows:

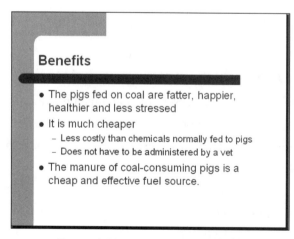

Figure 9.23: Demoted bullet points

9.13 Adding slide transitions

Transitions change the way that a slide opens. You can make the next slide open like a blind or a curtain, for example.

- Click the **Slide Sorter View** button at the bottom left of the screen.

You will notice that an extra Slide Sorter toolbar appears at the top of the screen. This has all the tools for adding transitions and effects to your slides.

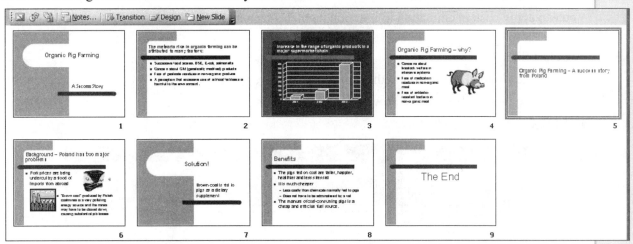

Figure 9.24: Slide Sorter view with toolbar

- First select the slides to which you want to apply the transition effect. Select Slide 1, and then hold down **Ctrl** while you select slides 2, 3, 4, 5, 7 and 8.
- Click the **Slide Transition** icon on the Slide Sorter toolbar.

A Slide Transition Task pane opens:

- Scroll down the list and select an effect – you can experiment to find a suitable one. This will apply the effect just to your selected slides.
- To apply the transition to all slides click the **Apply to All Slides** button.
- Change to Slide Show view and try out the result.

Figure 9.25

9.14 Adding animation to text and objects

- In Slide Sorter view select Slide 4.
- Click the **Design** button on the Slide Sorter toolbar. Click **Animation Schemes** in the Task pane and then select **Ascend**.
- Switch to Slide Show View to test the effect. You have to click the mouse button to make each picture or line of text appear.

You can apply custom animation to individual objects on a slide. To do this, you have to change to Normal view.

- Select Slide 6.
- Click the **Normal View** icon at the bottom left of the screen.
- From the menu select **Slide Show, Custom Animation**.
- Choose effects for each object.

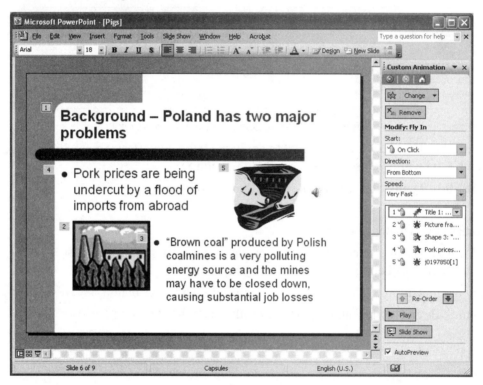

Figure 9.26: Adding custom animation

- Test out the effects. You may find the animation order seems wrong – if so, go back and alter it using the **Re-order** buttons in the Custom Animation Task pane.
- Save your presentation.
- EXPERIMENT!

9.15 Printing your slides

You will need to print out your slides to put in your portfolio. You may also want to give hard copy of a presentation to the audience.

You can print several slides to a page by selecting **Handouts**.

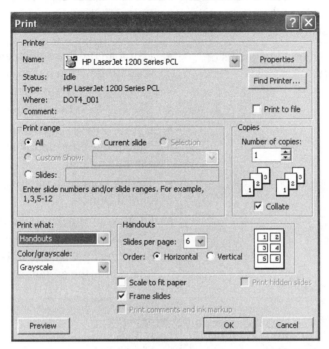

Figure 9.27: Printing slides

9.16 Delivery

Presentation skills are an important form of communication, and once learned will stand you in good stead all your life. Here are a few tips for a successful presentation:

♦ If you are giving the presentation using an overhead projector, make sure that you have set it up so that you can face the audience and refer to the screen behind or beside you.

♦ Double-check before the presentation that all the equipment is functioning correctly, and that the screen is visible from all seats in the room.

♦ Make sure the text on each screen is large enough to be read from all parts of the room.

♦ Introduce yourself and the topic to the audience. Keep your voice bright and enthusiastic, and try to look as if you are enjoying yourself.

♦ Don't rush – give the audience time to absorb what is on the screen, and what you are saying.

♦ Maintain eye contact with the audience. You can stop and ask a question now and then, to keep them involved.

♦ Always rehearse your presentation in advance so that you know exactly how long it will take.

9.17 Relating this chapter to the specification

Specification Reference (Part B)	What you have done to satisfy this
IT3.1	
Plan how to obtain and use the information required for your tasks	• Planning the presentation
Make selections based on judgements of relevance and quality.	• Using an on-line search engine and searching within a web site to find appropriate information and images • Use CD-ROM based image libraries • Use of library catalogues to find books containing information and images which can be scanned • Taking your own photographs using a digital camera • Draw your images / take photographs to be scanned • Selecting appropriate information and images for the audience
IT3.2	
Enter and bring together information using formats that help development	• Use of slide template • Use of bullet points • Inclusion of similar image types
Use software features to improve the efficiency of your work	• Production of charts
Annotate/document your work to show that you have understood the processes followed and have taken account of the views of others	• Group presentations • Rehearsing presentations
IT3.3	
Develop the presentation so it is accurate, clear and presented consistently, taking account of the views of others	• Modifying default text sizes • Changing the Design Template • Changing the colour scheme • Slide transition / animation
Present your final output effectively using a format and style that suits your purpose and audience.	• Use of multimedia (i.e. sound and animation) to maintain interest • Format and style appropriate for student audience • Spell-check and testing of the animation and transition • Rehearsal beforehand to seek the views of others

9.18 Other Key Skills signposting

Communication   C3.2b Make a formal presentation using at least one image

Application of Number   N3.3 Interpret results of your calculations, present your findings using a chart and justify your methods.

9.19 Evidence for your portfolio

There should be many opportunities in your main area of study for creating presentations. Some ideas include:

- a presentation based on one of your assignments (e.g. some historical research or a geographical field study)
- the presentation of survey results (e.g. a media survey on the T.V. viewing habits of teenagers)
- a presentation informing people about computer viruses
- a sales presentation to promote a new product
- a 'rolling' presentation for your school or college reception area providing information for visitors
- a presentation to raise awareness and support for your favourite charity

Type of evidence	✔
A written description of the activity	
An action plan for obtaining and using the information	
Hand-drawn sketches of the slides	
Print-outs of information retrieved from the Internet, including screenshots of search engines in use (you could annotate these with explanations of how you refined the search)	
Notes of any books referenced, or photographs scanned, refer to any copyright issues you encountered	
Printouts of earlier versions of the slides annotated with amendments to be made and why (e.g. results of spell-check, comments from others etc.)	
A final printout of the slides annotated with notes on animation and slide transition	
Final printouts of the slides	
Notes on the planning and role of each person involved in a group presentation	
Record from your assessor of how you developed and presented the presentation	

9.20 Sample questions

Task 1

1. Open PowerPoint and select the **Watermark** Template Design.
2. Create a title slide, with the main heading "SPACE" and the subheading "The Moon & Planets".
3. Centre the headings and adjust the text size to 72 and 48 respectively.
4. Make the subheading bold.
5. Insert a new slide to contain some text and Clip Art. Give it the title "The Earth's Moon".
6. Enter the following points:
   - 1/4 the size of the Earth
   - 1/6 the gravity of the Earth
   - Man first walked on the moon in 1969
7. Insert an appropriate picture for the topic from the Clip Art Gallery.
8. Create a new slide for the end of the presentation and insert the text "The End".
9. Print out all of the slides so that they all fit on one A4 page.

Task 2

1. Insert a new slide before the last slide. This will contain text and a chart.
2. Apply a different design to all of the slides.
3. Open Microsoft Excel and insert the following information in a new worksheet:

Planet	Average Distance from Sun (in millions of miles)
Earth	93
Jupiter	483
Mars	142
Mercury	36
Neptune	2793
Pluto	3670
Saturn	886
Uranus	1782
Venus	67

4. Sort the table by distance from the sun in ascending order.
5. Create a horizontal bar chart from the data. Include chart titles and a legend.
6. Import the chart into the new slide you created in PowerPoint.
7. Spell-check the presentation and check for accuracy.
8. Print out the slides so that they all fit on one A4 page.

Chapter 10 – Developing a Database Application

Objectives

- To learn how to plan and carry through a fairly large-scale activity
- To communicate with a user to discover their requirements in terms of input, processing and output
- To import data files
- To validate data entered by the user
- To customise a form for data input
- To refine queries so that the user can enter conditions at run time
- To customise reports constructed from the results of a search
- To create a menu which the user will use to select the required task, e.g. input data, perform a search and print a report, close the application
- To break down a project into a series of tasks and draw up a schedule for completion

10.1 Preparing for the Level 3 test

In the external test you will be required to create a specified database structure and to import data files provided by QCA. You may be asked to edit, sort and query the database records and to produce formatted reports. Make sure you are familiar with the techniques covered in Chapter 5 before tackling this chapter – these chapters cover most of the skills required for the database element of the test.

10.2 Choosing a suitable project for your portfolio

At this level, you are required to plan and carry through a fairly large-scale activity ('a major task') if you are using this for portfolio evidence. You could satisfy this requirement by completing a database project for a real user. You need to find an application that is not too complex to carry out in the allotted time, and document the process of interviewing the user and determining their requirements. Then you can plan how you are going to tackle the problem, break the project down into a series of tasks and schedule each activity.

This chapter will deal with a database that involves only a single table. If you pick a project more complex than this, you will need another book – try 'Successful ICT Projects in Access' by P.M. Heathcote, published by Payne-Gallway.

A list of ideas for projects is given in paragraph 10.15 at the end of this chapter.

10.3 Finding the information and planning the database

If you have made contact with a user who may have a suitable project for you to tackle, you should plan an interview with them to ascertain requirements. Have a list of questions prepared, and a notebook in which to write down the answers. You will find that preparing a list of questions in advance focuses your mind on what information is needed, and the interview is less likely to end up as a vague chat about unrealistic objectives. The evidence of planning and carrying out the interview needs to be put into your portfolio using the Information Seeking record sheet and the Planning record sheet.

The type of questions you need to ask are:

1. What are the objectives of the project?

2. What format does the input take? Are any input documents currently used, or do they need to be designed?

3. What validation can be carried out on the data?

4. How much data is there – just a few records, or hundreds? (You don't have to actually input hundreds of records for a project – it is enough to show that it works for about 20 records.)

5. What output is required? Does this need to be in the form of hard-copy reports, or is it to be viewed on screen, or both?

6. What processing is required? Do totals need to be calculated? Are subsets of the data to be found using queries? Does the data need to be sorted differently for different reports?

7. Does the project need to be completed by a particular date?

Note that if you are not using IT to carry out any information seeking then you must carry out another activity covering a different purpose that does use IT to search for information.

It is important that you discuss your progress with the user, showing them drafts of your work and seeking feedback on content, layout, format and style. When the project is complete you must ensure that the user agrees that the system meets their requirements.

> **Sample task: Create a customised application for holiday cottage bookings**

In this task we are going to use the database which you created in Chapter 5, developing it into a complete application including a customised menu screen which is displayed when the database is opened. Building this application will give you the skills that you need to plan and implement a project of your own and will prepare you for the external test.

Instead of just opening your database from Chapter 5 you will practise importing the data from a comma delimited text file, just as you will in the external test. The file is called **Cottages data.txt** and can be downloaded from www.payne-gallway.co.uk/ksit. You will need to download this file and save it in a suitable folder on your computer.

10.4 Importing the data file

- Open Access and create a new database called **NewCottages.mdb** in your **Holidays** folder.
- Select **File**, **Get External Data**, **Import**.
- In the Import dialogue box select **Text Files** in the Files of type box.

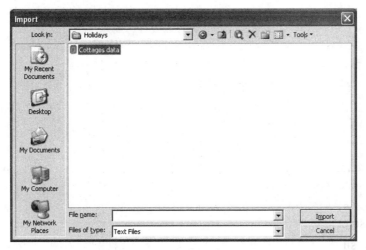

Figure 10.1: Importing the text file

- Navigate to the location of the text file **Cottages data.txt** and click **Import**.

The text file will be displayed in the Import Text Wizard window.

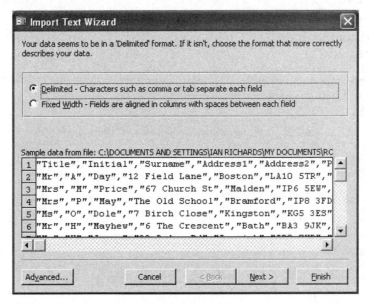

Figure 10.2: Choosing the format of the data

- Check the **Delimited** option and click **Next**.

The next step of the Import Text Wizard asks you for more formatting information.

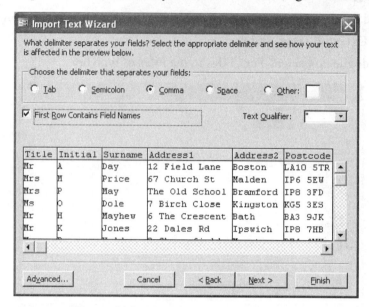

Figure 10.3: More formatting information

- Check the **Comma** option and also check the **First Row Contains Field Names** box. Click **Next**.

Now you are asked where you want to store the data.

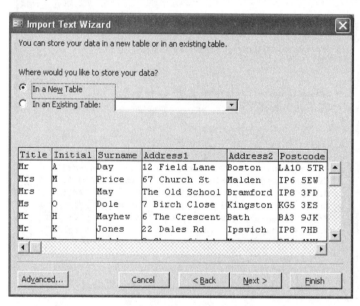

Figure 10.4: Specifying where to store the data

- Check the **In a New Table** option and click **Next**.

The data types for each field now have to be specified.

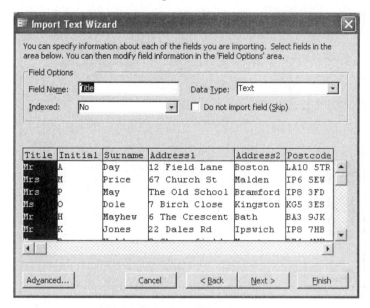

Figure 10.5: Specifying data types

- To specify the data types for the other fields click the **Advanced** button.

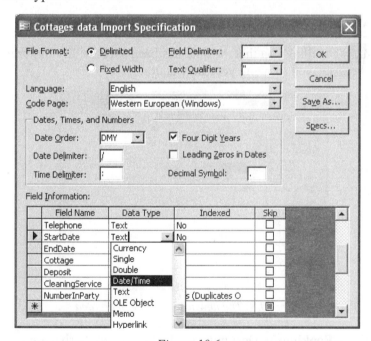

Figure 10.6

- Look back to Figure 5.7 and specify the data types given there.
- Click **OK** and then click **Next**.

You are now asked which field is the primary key.

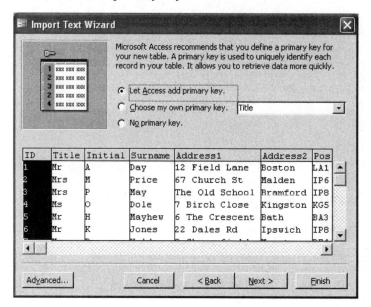

Figure 10.7: Setting the primary key

- Select the option **Let Access add primary key**. A new field called **ID** will be added. Click **Next**.

- In the final dialogue box enter the name *tblNewBookings* for the new table and click **Finish**.

You will receive a message telling you that the data has been successfully imported. The main Access window will be displayed showing your new table.

Figure 10.8: The new table has been created

- Open the table **tblNewBookings** in Design view. It should look fairly similar to your **Cottages.mdb** database from Chapter 5. You just need to rename the first field (the key field) as **BookingNumber**.

- If your Yes/No field is displaying words instead of the check boxes we had in the Cottages.mdb database, then in Design View click the **Lookup** tab in **Field Properties** for this field and change the Display Control to **Check Box**.

Before you sit the external test you should practise importing some of the sample data files provided by QCA.

Now we'll move on to develop this database into a complete application.

10.5 Validating input data

We are going to add default values, validation rules and error messages to various data fields as specified in the table below:

Field name	Default Value	Validation Rule	Validation Text
StartDate		Between 01/01/2004 and 31/12/2020	Please enter a date between 01/01/2004 and 31/12/2020
EndDate		Between 01/01/2004 and 31/12/2020	Please enter a date between 01/01/2004 and 31/12/2020
Cottage		Holly or Elm or Oak	Please enter Holly or Elm or Oak
Deposit	250	Between 100 and 300	Deposit must be between £100 and £300
NumberInParty	6	Between 1 and 6	Please enter a number between 1 and 6

Figure 10.9: Validation rules to be applied to the data

- In Design view click in the **StartDate** row. The table structure is displayed as shown below.

- Make sure the **General** tab is selected in the Field Properties pane at the bottom of the screen, as shown in Figure 10.10.

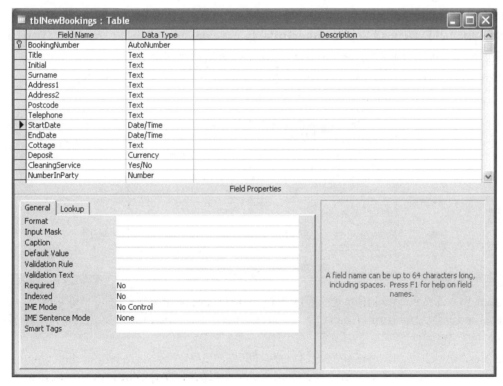

Figure 10.10: tblNewBookings in design view

- With the cursor in the **StartDate** field, type the validation rule and validation text in the appropriate rows exactly as shown in Figure 10.9.

- Move to the **EndDate** field and enter the validation rule and validation text.

- Enter the other validation rules as shown. Notice that **Deposit** and **NumberInParty** have been given a default value, since most customers are asked to pay a deposit of £250 and book for a party of 6.

- Save the table by clicking the **Save** icon.

- Switch to Datasheet view by clicking the **View** icon on the toolbar.

Because the table already contains data, you will see a warning message, as shown below.

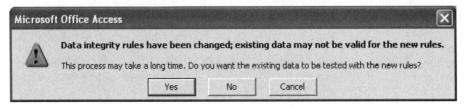

Figure 10.11: Access will check existing data

- If you have entered all the validation rules and default values correctly, the table will be saved. If not, you will see further error messages and you should check your validation rules are entered correctly. (It is also possible that you may have some existing invalid data in your table.)

- Try entering record 10 as shown below in Figure 10.12. As soon as you tab out of a field containing invalid data, an error message appears with your validation text. Note that the **EndDate** of 4/7/2004 is accepted although it is clearly an error – the validation rules do not say it must be after **StartDate**.

- Test out all the validations by entering invalid data.

- Note that the fields **Deposit** and **NumberInParty** have default values as specified. You can change these or leave them.

- Don't save the record – press **Esc** twice when you have finished experimenting.

- Close the table and return to the database window.

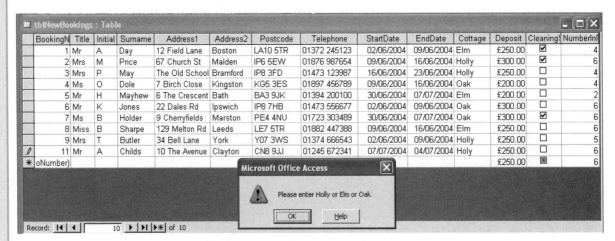

Figure 10.12: Validation rule applied

10.6 Designing a custom form for data entry

So far, all data has been entered in Datasheet view, as in Figure 10.12. While this is quite convenient when there are only a few fields in each record, and only a few records all of which are on the screen, for a larger, customised database it looks much more professional to enter data in a data entry 'form' specially created for this purpose.

- In the database window, click the **Forms** button and then select **Create form by using wizard**. Click **New**.

- In the next window, select **AutoForm: Columnar**. In the list box near the bottom of the screen, select **tblNewBookings** as the table or query where the object's data comes from, as in Figure 10.13.

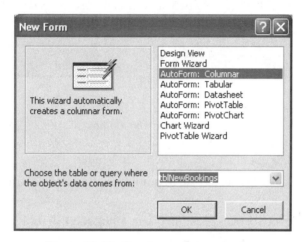

Figure 10.13: Creating a data entry form

- Click **OK**.

The form is created automatically, as shown below.

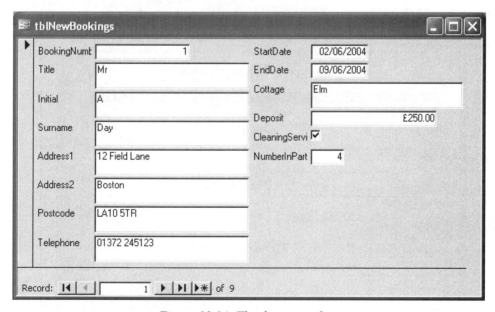

Figure 10.14: The data entry form

Customising the data entry form

You can alter almost all aspects of the data entry form. You can change the title in the title bar, change its background, rearrange the fields, give the form a heading, remove the record selectors, add custom buttons and so on. We will start by rearranging the fields and giving the form a heading.

Adding a heading and rearranging fields

- Click the **Design view** button on the toolbar to go to Design view.

- Make the window big enough so that you can see the whole form with some to spare.

- Click between the **Form Header** and **Detail** sections of the form and drag downwards to create some space in the form header section. (See Figure 10.16.)

- The Toolbox should be visible as shown below. If it is not, select **View, Toolbox** from the menu.

Pointer tool   Label tool

Figure 10.15: The toolbox

- Click the **Label** tool and drag out an area in the Form header.

- Enter the text *Cottage Bookings*. Make the text bold, centred and choose a suitable font and size.

- You can also give the textbox a background colour. Click the **Fill** tool in the Formatting toolbar and select a colour.

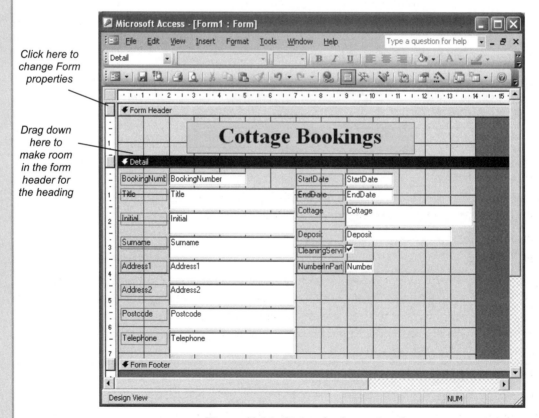

Figure 10.16: Giving the form a heading

- You can select multiple fields by selecting the **Pointer** tool on the toolbox and then dragging through or around the fields you want to select. Try selecting **StartDate**, **EndDate** and Cottage. The cursor changes to a hand and you can drag them down to the bottom of the form as shown below in Figure 10.17. Do the same with **Deposit**, **CleaningService** and **NumberInParty**.

- Select the fields **Title** and **Initial** and make them much shorter.

- Select all the fields from **Surname** to **Telephone** and make them shorter.

- Move **Initial** and **Surname** as shown below.

- Size the field labels appropriately.

- Select the labels in the first column by 'lassoing' them and right-justify them by clicking the **Right Align** button on the Formatting toolbar.

- Similarly, right align the other labels.

- You can move a field separately from its label by dragging its top left-hand corner. See if you can arrange and size the fields so that the form looks something like the one below, viewed in Form View. (You can move a selected field when the mouse pointer changes to a hand.)

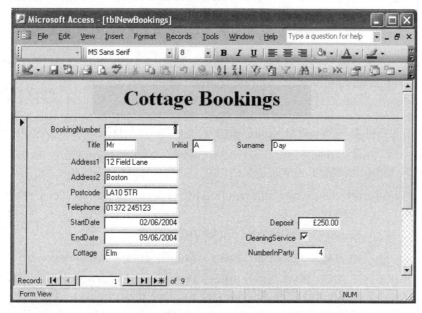

Figure 10.17: The fields rearranged on the form

(**Note**: You can reorder the records at any time in Datasheet view by placing the cursor in the column you want to sort on and pressing the **Sort Ascending** button.)

- Save the form, naming it *frmBooking*.

The Properties box

The form and each object on it (label, textbox, and other objects which you could place on the form such as buttons, list boxes, etc) have a set of properties which determine its appearance, colour, size, behaviour etc. By changing the properties of an object you can control its format, as well as any events that happen when, for example, it is clicked or double-clicked, opened or closed, tabbed into or out of.

- Return to Design view.

- Right-click anywhere in the form to display a shortcut menu and select **Properties**.

- Click in the corner at the intersection of the ruler lines. This selects the Form, so that you can change its properties. (See Figure 10.18.)

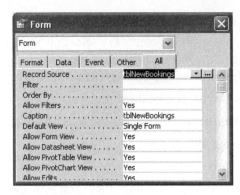

Figure 10.18: The Form Properties sheet

- With the **Format** tab selected, change the **Caption** Property from *tblNewBookings* to *Cottage Bookings*. Test out the change in Form view; the caption in the Title bar at the top of the form has changed.

- You can experiment with different properties then save and close the form to return to the database window.

10.7 Advanced queries

In Chapter 5 you designed and saved two queries named **qryHolly&Elm**, and **qryHolly&ElmSorted**. You can return to **Cottages.mdb**, open each of these queries in Design view and then run them to remind yourself how they work. Now return to the database you have been working on this chapter – **NewCottages.mdb**.

In this section we are going to design a query that allows the user to enter the name of a cottage and then find all the bookings for that cottage.

- In the **NewCottages.mdb** database window, click the **Queries** button, select **Create query in Design view** and click **New**.

- Click **Design view** in the next window, and click **OK**.

- Click **Add** to add **tblNewBookings** to the Query window. Then click **Close**.

- Double-click each of the fields **BookingNumber**, **Title**, **Initial**, **Surname**, **StartDate**, **EndDate**, **Cottage**, **Deposit** and **CleaningService** to place these fields on the query grid.

- In the **Criteria** row for **Cottage**, type *[Please enter Cottage:]*.

- In the **Sort** row for **StartDate**, select **Ascending**.

The query should look like Figure 10.19.

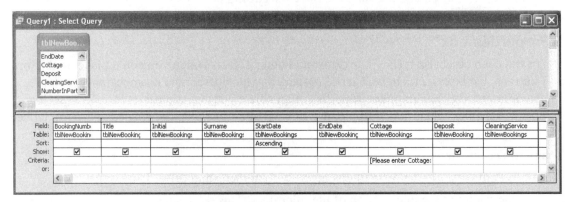

Figure 10.19: A criteria to be entered at run time

- Save the query as **qryCottage**.
- Run the query. A dialogue box appears as shown below:

Figure 10.20: Criteria dialogue box

- Type *Holly* and click **OK**. The query now runs, showing all the bookings for Holly Cottage.

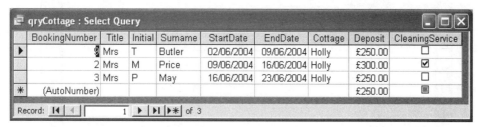

Figure 10.21: Query results table

- Save and close the query.

10.8 Creating and customising reports

Customised reports can be created from Queries or Tables. We will make a report based on the query **qryCottage** that we have just created. Reports can take various formats so we will start by looking at a columnar format.

- From the database window select **Reports, Create report in Design view** and click **New**.
- In the next window select **AutoReport: Columnar** and select **qryCottage** in the lower list box. Click **OK**.
- The first thing that happens is that the query runs and a dialogue box opens asking you to enter a cottage name. Type *Holly* and click **OK**.

The report wizard then creates a report as shown below in Figure 10.22.

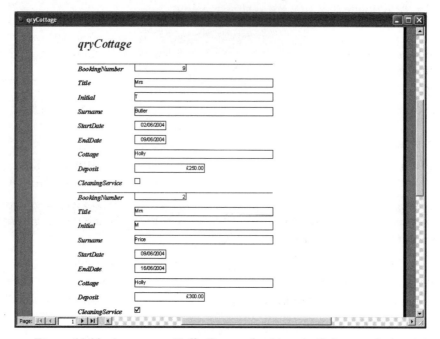

Figure 10.22: A report on Holly Cottage bookings in Columnar format

This report format is not really suitable: if there were a lot of bookings it would take up an awful lot of paper and it is hard to see at a glance what dates are not booked. We will take a look at a different format.

- Close the report without saving it and return to the Database window.
- Select **Reports, Create report in Design view** and click **New**.
- In the next window select **AutoReport: Tabular** and select **qryCottage** in the lower list box. Click **OK**.
- Type *Holly* in the dialogue box asking you to enter the name of a cottage.

This time the report appears as in Figure 10.23 – a slightly more promising start.

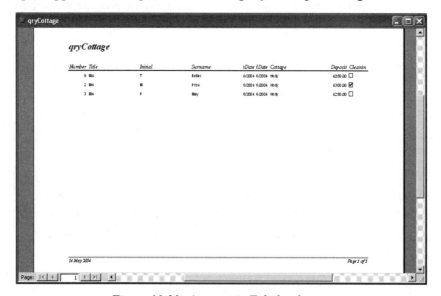

Figure 10.23: A report in Tabular format

The report is shown in Landscape view. It needs several modifications – for example:

♦ It needs a proper heading, not one which says **qryCottage** (the query on which the report is based.)

♦ The first and last fields are falling off the edge of the report – the field widths and labels could be made much narrower so that it fits neatly on the page.

♦ The name **Holly** does not need to appear in every single row – this is a report on Holly Cottage bookings and the cottage name could be shown just once at the top of the report.

- Switch to Design view.
- Click in the **Report Header** box and change the heading from **qryCottage** to **Cottage Bookings**.
- Click in the label **Title**. Hold down the **Shift** key while you select the **Title** field underneath the label, the label **Initial** and the field **Initial**. Drag the right handle to the left on any of the selected objects to make them narrower.
- Move the selected boxes to the right and make the **BookingNumber** label and field wider to accommodate the whole heading.
- Select the label and field for **Surname** and move them left. Do the same for **StartDate** and **EndDate**.

Your report should now look something like the one below:

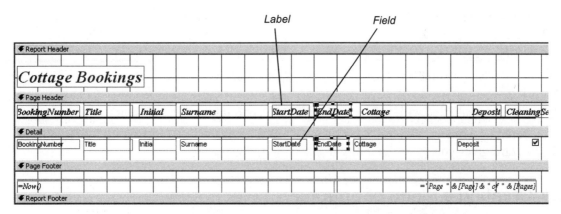

Figure 10.24: Customising the report

- Switch to Print Preview to view your changes. The report looks better already.
- Go back to Design view.
- Drag the field **Cottage** into the **Report Header** area. (See Figure 10.24.)
- You may not be able to drag the label; if not, cut it and then click in the Report Header area before pasting it. Move it next to the field.
- Make both the field and the label size **20** points to match the heading.
- Select the label and field and hold down **Shift** while you select the report heading. Select **Format, Align, Bottom** from the menu to line up the three objects accurately.
- Select the fields and labels for **Deposit** and **CleaningService** and drag them to the left.
- Make other minor adjustments to object sizes and alignment.

The report format should now look like Figure 10.25.

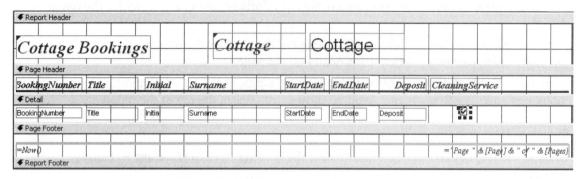

Figure 10.25: The customised report layout

- Click the **Print Preview** button to view your report. It should look like Figure 10.26.

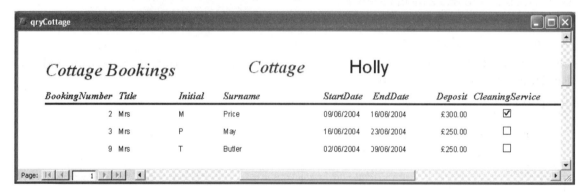

Figure 10.26: The finished report

- When you are satisfied with your report, save it as **rptBookings** and close it.
- You could experiment with using the Report wizard to create a report from **tblNewBookings**. The wizard gives you more flexibility in selecting fields for the report.

10.9 Creating a menu of options

Now comes the fun bit! You can create a front-end menu from which the user can select options. The menu that we will create will have just three options: **Enter a Booking**, **Print Report**, and **Exit Database**.

Access has a special tool called the **Switchboard Manager** to create a front-end menu (referred to as a Switchboard in Access).

- To start the Switchboard Manager, select **Tools, Database Utilities, Switchboard Manager**.

You will see a message:

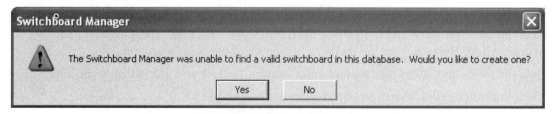

Figure 10.27: Creating a new switchboard

- Click **Yes**. The Switchboard Manager automatically adds a page called **Main Switchboard (Default)** to its window.

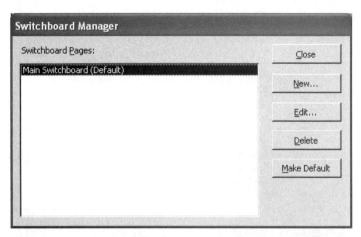

Figure 10.28: Adding a new item to the switchboard

Note: Any time you want to display this window in order to edit your switchboard, select **Tools, Database Utilities, Switchboard Manager**.

Creating the main switchboard

- Click **Edit** to edit the main switchboard. (If you had a more complex menu structure that called other menus, you would need to add new menu pages.)
- In the Edit Switchboard Page window, click **New** to add the first item to the switchboard.
- When the user selects this option from the menu, you want the customised form **frmBooking** that you created in paragraph 10.6 to open ready to add a new record. Make entries as shown below in Figure 10.29.

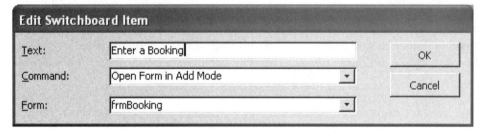

Figure 10.29: Defining a menu item

- Click **OK**.
- Back in the Edit Switchboard Page window, click **New** to add the second item to the menu.
- In the Edit Switchboard Item window, enter the text **Print Report**. In the second box, select the command **Open report**, and in the third box select the report **rptBookings**. Click **OK**.
- In the Edit Switchboard Page window, click **New** to add the third and final item to the menu.
- In the Edit Switchboard Item window, enter the text **Exit Database**. In the second box, select the command **Exit Application**. Click **OK**.
- Click **Close** in the **Edit Switchboard Page** window.
- Click **Close** in the **Switchboard Manager** window. You will be returned to the Database window.

Testing and editing the switchboard

- Click the **Forms** button, select **Switchboard** and click **Open**.

The menu opens as shown below in Figure 10.30.

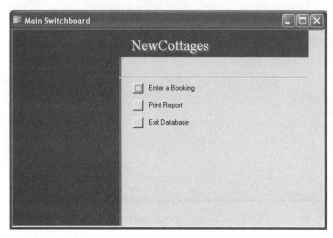

Figure 10.30: The main menu (switchboard)

- Test each of the menu items in turn.
- If anything is not working correctly, select **Tools, Database Utilities, Switchboard Manager** again and edit your switchboard.
- The Properties window probably opens when you display the switchboard for the first time. In Design view, you can change the properties of any object including the form itself.

Adding a graphic

- Go to Design view.
- Click in the green part of the form and look at the Properties box. (If it is not visible, right-click the form and select **Properties**.)
- Click the **All** tab and select **Picture**. Click the three dots beside the line and a dialogue box appears asking you to choose a picture. You will find some in a folder called *Program Files\Microsoft Office\Office11\ Bitmaps\Dbwiz*.

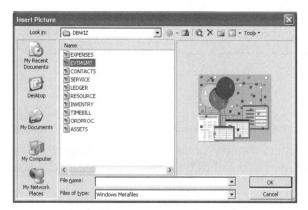

Figure 10.31: Inserting a graphic.

- Choose a suitable graphic (well, the best of a bad lot) and click **OK**.

The graphic is inserted. It does not fit very well and you will have to play around with it to get a reasonable result.

10.10   Creating an Autoexec macro

When the user opens the application, the database window is displayed and the user has to select **Forms**, **Switchboard**, **Open** to display the menu. It would be preferable to have the menu appear automatically when the application opens. To achieve this you need to create a **macro**. A macro is a sequence of one or more instructions that is executed when some event occurs.

Any macro that is named **AutoExec** will execute automatically as soon as the database is loaded. We will create one that minimises the database window and opens the Switchboard form.

- In the Database window click **Macros** and click **New**.

- Enter the two commands as shown below, setting **Switchboard** as the form name.

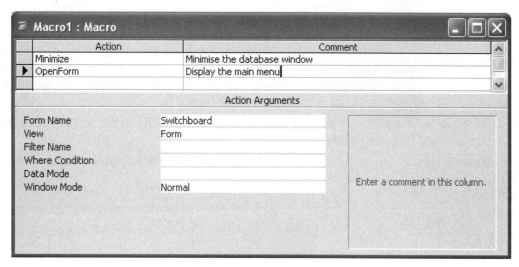

Figure 10.32: Creating an AutoExec macro

- Save the macro, naming it *AutoExec*.

- Close the macro window, and close the database.

- Open the database again. The switchboard should appear automatically.

That completes the sample project. You are now ready to tackle one of your own!

10.11   Breaking down the project into a series of tasks

When you tackle a fairly large-scale activity, you need to write down all the tasks that are involved in completing it and plan how much time you can afford to spend on each one. It may be difficult to stick to the plan but that does not mean you don't need one. At least you will be aware when you are falling behind and need to get up before midday for a few weeks.

The tasks involved in completing the sample project would probably include:

1. Looking for a suitable project.

2. Interviewing a user to determine their requirements.

3. Documenting their requirements.

4. Implementing the database, trying out different options for say Forms and Reports and documenting why you chose a particular format or method.

5. Consulting the user during the implementation process, to make sure you are on the right track, and making adjustments or improvements where suggested.

6. Testing the database with carefully chosen test data.

7. Going back to the user and getting them to test it, give their opinion and make suggestions for improvement.

8. Acting on those suggestions.

9. Writing a user manual using a word processing package.

10. Putting the whole project together with a Table of Contents, ready to add to your portfolio.

11. Keeping a log as you go along of what you are doing, problems encountered, how you solved them.

10.12   Drawing up a schedule for completing the project

You will know how many weeks are available for completing the task you have set yourself. Make a plan of what you are going to do each week. If time is to be spent at school or College on the project, make sure you plan activities that can be completed in those times regardless of whether or not you have been able to find a user or interview them, or whether you have started the application at home in a different version of the software. You can spend time experimenting with the software, writing up notes, creating a template for a user manual and so on.

You may have a computer at home on which you plan to do the majority of the work. That's fine – but don't waste the time that you are given in class.

The schedule can be added to your portfolio as evidence of your ability to plan and carry through the project. A sample schedule is shown below.

Week Number (or date)	Activity	Notes
1	Interview user. Write up notes of interview. Document requirements.	
2	Design database table, decide what forms, reports, queries, macros and menus are needed.	
3	Start implementation.	
4	Continue implementation. Check progress with user to make sure that requirements were correctly understood.	
5	Finish implementation.	
6	Test database. Ask user to test it.	
7	Make improvements and finish documentation.	
8	Write user manual and include screenshots of application as evidence.	
9	Put everything together. Create table of contents. Put it in the portfolio.	
10	Demonstrate to moderator.	

Figure 10.33: A sample schedule

10.13   Relating this chapter to the specification

Specification Reference (Part B)	What you have done to satisfy this
IT3.1	
Plan how to obtain and use the information required for your tasks	• Planning an interview • Schedule for completing the project
Make selections based on judgements of relevance and quality.	• Conducting the interview • Identify data for input • Identify existing data input forms or design • Selecting appropriate information for inclusion in database • Design of database record structure
IT3.2	
Enter and bring together information using formats that help development	• Production of table • Validation of database entries • Reports generated from the database
Use software features to improve the efficiency of your work	• Data entry form • Queries on the database • Sorting information • Autoexec macro • Production of reports based on queries • (User manual & mail merge – Chapter 11)
Annotate/document your work to show that you have understood the processes followed and have taken account of the views of others	• Discussing drafts of your work with the user during the project
IT3.3	
Develop the presentation so it is accurate, clear and presented consistently, taking account of the views of others	• Creation of front end menu • Customising forms • Customising reports
Present your final output effectively using a format and style that suits your purpose and audience.	• Consulting the user • Autoexec macro – menu appears automatically for user • Data input forms provide an effective user interface • Appropriate format and style of reports • Validation routines • Acting on comments from user

10.14 Other Key Skills signposting

Communication C.3.2a Take part in a group discussion.

10.15 Evidence for your portfolio

In choosing a database, you will be wise to stick to something fairly simple which involves only one table. A suitable project could for example be based around one of the following ideas:

♦ Keeping records of members of a Club or Society. Names, addresses, subscription, type of member etc. can be recorded. This could also involve a mail merge (see Chapter 11).

♦ A list of customers, jobs, goods or invoices for a small business can be held in a database. Details of each customer or job can be entered and suitable processing tasks carried out.

♦ A database of pets at a vet's surgery can be used to send out reminders to the owners for vaccinations etc.

♦ A list of sports fixtures, giving dates, locations, opposing team, location, scores etc.

♦ Student records giving name, address, date of birth, year group, tutor group etc.

Type of evidence	✔
A written description of the activity	
An action plan for obtaining and using the information (e.g. questions to ask the user, schedule of tasks to be completed)	
A record of the interview with the user	
Copies of any input documents previously in use	
Printout of field properties	
Notes on queries and reports to be generated and why	
Working drafts of menu, tables, forms, queries and reports annotated with amendments to be made and why (e.g. comments from user etc.)	
Printouts (or screenshots) of input form showing validation rules in action	
A final printout (or screenshots) of menu, tables, forms, queries and reports	
A copy of the user manual (see Chapter 11)	
Record from your assessor of how you developed and presented the project	

10.16 Sample questions

You work for a Tourist Information Centre that wishes to set up a computerised database of the hotels in the local area. This information needs to include details of the accommodation and facilities at each of the hotels so that enquiries from the public can be dealt with efficiently.

Task 1

1. Create a new database using a suitable file name.
2. Create a table and save it as *tblHotelDetails*.

3.   Create a structure for the table with the field titles shown below. Use appropriate data types for each field.

4.   Enter the following details:

Name	Postcode	Bedrooms	Dogs	Lowest Price
The Glenbrook	IP16 4FG	45	N	£55.00
Ryans Guest House	IP4 6DF	12	Y	£25.00
Midsommer House	IP7 9KL	24	N	£32.50
The Park	IP1 8YH	86	Y	£75.00
Chelston Towers	IP8 6YU	67	N	£65.00
High Hall	IP13 8CV	18	N	£42.00
Parkside Guest House	IP9 7MN	7	Y	£18.00
The Tythe Arms	IP1 6DF	14	N	£28.00
St. James	IP12 9DV	37	N	£68.00
Siddington Hall	IP4 7AS	56	N	£98.00
Ambury House	IP3 4VB	10	N	£58.00

5.   Check for accuracy and print out a copy.

6.   Add the details of two hotels which have just opened. Their details are as follows:
Larkspur Hill House, IP16 9KL. It has 26 bedrooms, does not accept dogs and the lowest price per room is £45.00.
The Naresborough, IP2 8UJ. It has 12 bedrooms, does not accept dogs and the lowest price is £35.00.

7.   Sort all the records by Lowest Price in ascending order.

8.   Check for accuracy, save your work and print out a copy.

Task 2

1.   From the table select those hotels which accept dogs and have a lowest price less than £50.00.

2.   Print out the results of this selection in report format, giving it an appropriate title. Include your name and today's date in the footer.

3.   Return to the full list of records.

4.   Arrange the columns so that the postcode is in the last column and remove the 'Dogs' column.

5.   Print out this information in report format, again with an appropriate title. Include your name and today's date in the footer.

Chapter 11 – Further Word Processing Techniques

Objectives

- ❑ To use an existing template for sending business letters
- ❑ To create and save a new customised letter template
- ❑ To create a mail-merge letter and merge it with selected names and addresses from a list stored in a database
- ❑ To write a user manual for a customised application using styles, headers and footers, screenshots, automatic table of contents

11.1 Choosing a suitable project and determining user requirements

If you choose a word processing activity to present as part of your evidence then you must demonstrate that you have produced the documents for a particular purpose, preferably for an identified user. You must therefore discuss the requirements of the project with the user before you begin and consult them for their views on content, layout, format and style while your work is in progress. Notes of these discussions should be recorded and submitted as evidence.

A suitable project, using the activities described in this chapter, could for example be based around one of the following ideas.

- ◆ Producing a set of templates for a company's stationery
- ◆ Setting up a company mailshot using mail merge
- ◆ Producing a document, incorporating diagrams and pictures, e.g. a User Manual
- ◆ Word processing can often be integrated with one of the other activities, for example to create documentation for a database system or to prepare text for a desk top publishing application.

11.2 Finding information and planning the documents

Depending on the word processing project that you decide to undertake you may use IT to search for information by using the Internet or reference CD-ROMs. Alternatively information might be provided by the user, for example the logo and company details to include on company stationery. If you are not using IT to carry out any information seeking then you must carry out another activity covering a different purpose that does use IT to search for information. Record your sources on an Information Seeking record sheet (a sample is provided at www.payne-gallway.co.uk/ksit.) in your portfolio.

Before you start using the word processing software it is a good idea to plan the layout of the documents by drawing rough sketches by hand. Include this as evidence in your portfolio along with a Planning record sheet.

11.3 Using an existing template

A **template** is a preformatted document to which you add text of your own. The headed stationery that a school or college uses, or a blank invoice form, are examples of templates.

When you create a new Word document using the **New** command from the **File** menu, the Task pane opens and you can select either **New Blank document** which will open a new document with the default **Normal** template, or you can search for a different template.

Figure 11.1: Opening a new document

Word offers a range of templates which contain preset information and styles for various different documents you might want to compose.

For example, if you click **On my computer** in the **Templates** section and click the **Letters and Faxes** tab, you are given the following options:

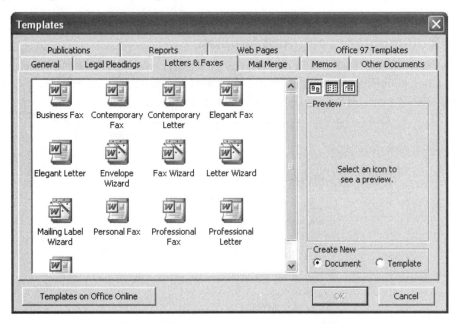

Figure 11.2: Letters and Faxes templates

Notice that you now have the choice of opening either a **Document** or a **Template**. If you want to use one of the templates to create your own letter, fax cover sheet or envelope, select **Document**. If you want to edit the actual template and save it under a different name as your own personalised template, choose **Template**.

You can create a new template in several ways:

♦ Select **New from Template**, select an existing template, edit and save it. To edit an existing template, you must open it *as a template*, make the changes you want and then save it as a template (with a *.dot* extension) under the same or a different name.

♦ Select **New Blank Document**, open a new document and add all the boilerplate text and graphics that you want to appear in the template. Then save it as a Document template (**.dot** file). (*Boilerplate* text is simply text such as a letterhead that appears in every document based on the template.)

♦ A variation on the second method is to open any existing document, delete anything that you do not want to appear in the template, and save it with a **.dot** extension.

Sample task: Use and edit an existing template for a letter

This task has two parts to it. Firstly, you will use an existing template to write a letter as follows:

• Open a new document using one of Word's existing templates.

• Try out the various features of the template.

• Type a short letter using the template.

• Save the letter as *Confirmation Mrs Day.doc*, and close the document.

Secondly, you will edit the actual template, save it as a new template and then try it out, as follows:

• Open the Word template *as a template*.

• Customise it to your requirements.

• Save it as *Highland Letterhead.dot*.

• Open a new document using this template and type a short letter.

Using the Contemporary Letter.dot template

• Select **File, New**. In the Task pane click **On my computer** and then click the **Letters and Faxes** tab. Choose *Contemporary Letter* and click **OK** to open it as a document.

The template will appear on the screen as shown in Figure 11.3.

Figure 11.3: The Contemporary Letter template

- Click where indicated to type in a new company name, address and slogan – you can make one up.

- Type the recipient's name and address, e.g. *Mrs A. Day*.

- Click on *Dear Sir or Madam* with the right mouse button. This brings up several alternative greetings, none of which are suitable. Delete the greeting and type *Dear Mrs Day*.

- Type a short letter in place of the existing text, confirming Mrs Day's booking of Elm Cottage from June 2nd to June 9th.

- Type your name at the bottom of the letter. It will appear something like Figure 11.4.

15 Dock Street
Ipswich
IP2 7GE

Highland Holidays Ltd

May 12, 2004

Mrs A Day
12 Field Lane
Boston LA10 5TR

Dear Mrs Day

Thank you for booking with Highland Holidays, and for your deposit of £250. Your booking of Elm Cottage for a party of four from June 2nd to June 6th is confirmed.

Yours sincerely

Amanda Peters
Director

Figure 11.4: A letter typed using the Contemporary Letter template

- Save the letter as *Confirmation Mrs Day.doc* and close it.

What you have just done is to use an existing template to create your own letter. However, you have not changed the actual template.

11.4 Editing an existing template

The next stage is to customise the template so that you do not have to retype your own company name, address, etc every time you want to type a letter.

- Select **File**, **New**. In the Task pane click **On my computer** and then click the **Letters and Faxes** tab. Choose *Contemporary Letter* and this time, select **Template** before you click **OK**.

The template will appear on the screen as shown in Figure 11.3.

- Click where indicated to type in a new company name, address and slogan as shown in Figure 11.4.

- Edit the closing so that instead of *Sincerely* it reads *Yours sincerely* which sounds less American.

- Add your name and the title **Director**.

Creating a new text style

The template contains several different text styles. Click on various parts of the letter such as the opening, body and closing. Although the styles have different names they are all Times New Roman 10pt. There is not really any need to have so many styles in your customised template. We will create a new style for the whole letter called **Letter Text**.

- Select the whole letter from the date down to the job title **Director**.
- Click in the **Font Size** box on the Formatting toolbar and select **12**.
- Click in the Style box on the standard toolbar and type *Letter text*. Press **Enter**.

Editing an existing style

When writing a business letter it is common practice to state the subject of the letter immediately below the greeting. The template already has a style called Subject line, which we will edit. The new **Subject Line** style will be 12 point Times Roman, bold, underlined and centred.

- After *Dear Sir or Madam* at the head of the letter, press **Enter**.
- Type the text *Subject of letter*.
- Click in the **Style** box to bring up a list of styles in the template, and scroll down to select **Subject Line** style.
- Reformat this line of text as **12 point Times Roman, bold, underlined** and **centred**.
- Click the **Subject Line** style again and press **Enter**. A dialogue box appears asking if you want to alter the style, or revert to the original Subject Line style.

Figure 11.5: Updating a style

- Leave **Update the style to reflect recent changes** and click **OK**.
- Try changing the **Return address** style to **12 point Times Roman**. (The return address is in the text box at the top of the page.)
- Click away from the text box when you have changed the format of the address.

11.5 Saving and using your template

- Save the amended template as *Highland Letterhead.dot*. If you are using a network with restricted rights, you will have to change the default destination drive and directory. If you are working at home, save the template in the default **Templates** directory.

If you are working at home, and have stored the template in the default location for templates, *C:\Windows\Application Data\Microsoft \Templates*
you will now be able to try out your template by selecting **File**, **New** from the menu and specifying your new template as the one to use (it will probably be put in the General templates category).

However, if you are working on a school or college network, you will now have a problem! You are not given the option to use a template stored in any other directory. You can use the following method.

Using a template stored on the A: drive

- Click the **Show Desktop** icon at the bottom left of the screen.
- From the desktop double-click on **My Computer**.
- Double-click on **A:** or wherever your template is stored.
- Right-click on *Highland Letterhead.dot* and select **New**. A new document based on the template will appear on your screen.
- Try using your template to type a short letter to Mrs Day informing her that the balance of £250.00 is now due for the holiday cottage rental. Save it as *Balance Due (Day).doc*, and close it.

11.6 Performing a mail merge

Mail merge is the term used for merging a list of names and addresses with a standard letter to create personalised letters. It's a very useful technique whenever you want to send the same letter to several people – for example,

- to let customers know about a new product or service;
- to chase overdue invoices;
- to remind members to pay their club or magazine subscriptions;
- to send letters to all the people who send YOU junk mail asking to be removed from their mailing lists.

In the Level 3 test you might be required to carry out a mail merge using a letter and data file supplied by QCA. The sample task below covers most of the skills required for this element of the test.

In the last chapter you created a database application to handle the bookings for 3 holiday cottages. One task that you might want to do, if you were the owner of the business, is to mail all your customers once a year to send them the latest catalogue and encourage them to book again. You can insert the names and addresses of all (or a selection) of the customers into a personalised letter.

> **Sample task:** Create a letter containing merge fields and merge the letter and data source to create personalised letters

For this task you will need the database **NewCottages.mdb** which was developed in Chapter 10. If you have not got it, you can download it from the web site www.payne-gallway.co.uk/ksit. Make sure you know which folder the database is saved in.

11.7 Creating the form letter

- Open a new document using the template **Highland Letterhead.dot** as described in paragraph 11.3.
- Select **Tools, Letters and Mailings, Mail Merge ...** from the menu. The Mail Merge Task pane is displayed as shown in Figure 11.6.

Figure 11.6: Creating a mail merge letter

- Select **Letters**, then click **Next**.

Step 2 of the mail merge asks you to select a starting document:

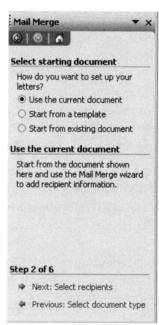

Figure 11.7: Selecting a starting document

- Select **Use the current document** and then click **Next**.

Step 3 asks you to select the recipients of the mail merge:

Figure 11.8: Selecting a data source

- Select **Use an existing list** and then click **Browse.**
- In the **Select Data Source** dialogue box, navigate to the folder containing NewCottages.mdb.
- Select **Access Databases** in the **Files of type** list box and select **NewCottages.mdb**. (See Figure 11.9.)

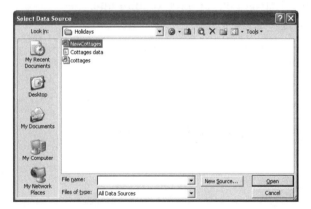

Figure 11.9: Specifying an Access database as the data source

Another dialogue box opens as shown below. (If a Properties window opens, close it.)

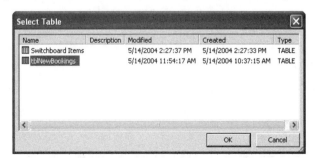

Figure 11.10: Selecting the table containing the names and addresses

- Select **tblNewBookings** and click **OK**.

The contents of the database table will be displayed, allowing you to edit the records if you wish.

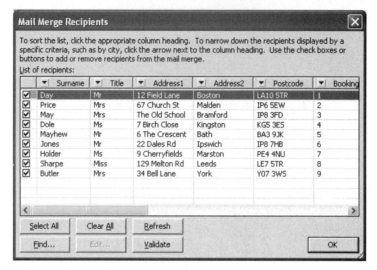

Figure 11.11: The mail merge recipients from tblNewBookings

- Click **OK** and return to the Mail Merge Task pane. Click **Next**.

In Step 4 you need to enter the recipient information into merge fields in your starting document.

- In the letter click on the field for recipient's address.

- In the Task pane click on **Address Block** and choose an appropriate format from the Insert Address Block window. Repeat this for the **Greeting line**.

- Type the letter as shown in Figure 11.12.

Figure 11.12: The mail merge letter

- To see what the letters will look like, click the arrows in Step 5 on the Mail Merge Task pane.

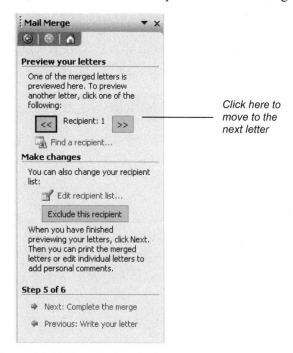

Click here to move to the next letter

Figure 11.13: Previewing the letters

Return to the first letter for Mr Day. You can see that the address is very spaced out. This is because we changed the style in the letter template to **Letter Text**, which has spacing between paragraphs. In retrospect maybe this was a mistake. We can put it right for this letter. Some other time, you would need to edit the actual template so that the style used for the address lines is more appropriate, with no spacing between address lines.

Changing paragraph spacing

- Select the name and the first three lines of the address, and on the menu select **Format, Paragraph**. The following dialogue box is displayed.

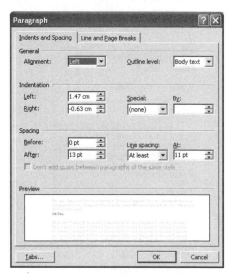

Figure 11.14: Formatting paragraphs

- Change the **Spacing After** to **0** and press **OK**.

Your first letter should look like Figure 11.15.

Figure 11.15: The letter merged with the first customer's details

- Click **Next** in the Mail Merge Task pane. This final step allows you to complete the merge. Before you do this, save the form letter as **New Catalogue.doc**.

11.8 Merging the data with the form letter

Now it's time to merge all the data in the database table with the form letter, so that the individual letters can be printed out (or viewed on screen).

- In Step 6 of the mail merge click **Edit individual letters**.

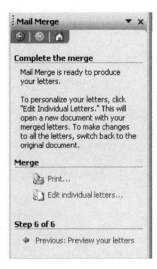

Figure 11.16: Completing the merge

The following window is displayed:

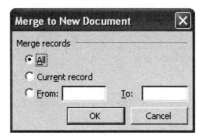

Figure 11.17: Merging the data

Note that you could select individual records to merge. We will merge all the records this time.

- Select **All** to merge all the records.

The first letter appears on screen. You can scroll down to see the other letters.

- If you want to print a sample letter, select **File, Print** and select **Current Page** in the dialogue box.

- Close **Letters1** without saving the document. There is no need to save the merged letters.

11.9 Selecting customers

Sometimes you may want to send letters to selected customers only. Suppose you wanted to send a letter only to those customers who have booked Holly Cottage in June, to inform them that the road to the cottage has been washed away by severe flooding but that they can they can be offered alternative bookings in Elm or Oak Cottage.

- With the Form letter **New Catalogue** open on your screen, select **File, Save As** to save the letter as *Flood Letter.doc*.

- Edit the letter with some suitable text. Include **<<Cottage>>** as a merged field somewhere in the letter, as shown in Figure 11.18. The easiest way to add this is to click in the appropriate place in the letter and then to use the Mail Merge toolbar. Display this by selecting **View, Toolbars, Mail Merge**. Click on the **Insert Merge Fields** button and choose **Cottage** from the list.

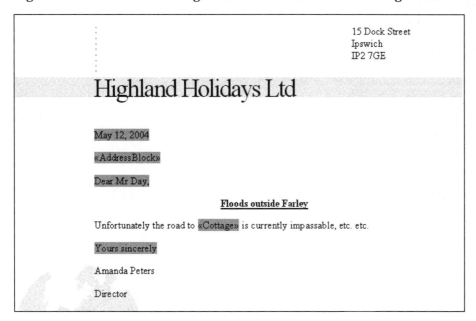

Figure 11.18: A new letter to be merged

- Return to Step 3 of the mail merge in the Task pane and select **Edit recipient list**.
- Click on the down arrow next to the column header **Cottage** and select **Holly** from the list

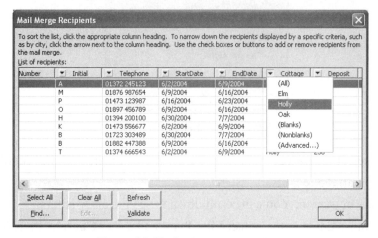

Figure 11.19: Setting query options

- Click **OK**.

The data has now been filtered to show only those bookings for Holly Cottage.

- Work through the remaining mail merge steps again in the Task pane and letters will just be produced for the people who have bookings for Holly Cottage.

That completes the Mail Merge exercise.

Sample task: Create a user manual for a customised software application

---

In the next exercise, you will create the beginnings of a user manual for a customised software application like the one described in Chapter 10.

A user manual needs a title page, a table of contents, and clear descriptions of how to use the application. Every page should have a page number and perhaps the title at the top or bottom of the page.

11.10 Creating a Style sheet

You need to set up various styles for chapter or section headings, paragraph headings, body text, figure numbers for screenshots, headers and footers. Although this set-up process is quite time-consuming it will pay dividends because it saves time in the long run and also ensures that your document has a consistent appearance throughout. You cannot create an automatic Table of Contents if you have not defined styles for the headings that you want to appear in the TOC.

- Open a new blank document.
- Look in the **Style** box at the styles that come with the **Normal** template – **Heading 1**, **Heading 2**, **Heading 3**, **Normal** etc.

You have a choice of whether to use the existing styles, edit them to your liking or create new ones for the user manual. It is a good idea to plan the styles that you need and describe them on a style sheet. This can then be used as a reference when creating your styles and using them.

For example, you could create the following styles for your user manual.

Style name	Use	Font	Following style	Size	Style	Justifi-cation	Space before	Space After
Title	Title page	Times New Roman	Title	36	Bold	Centre	36	0
Section	Section head	Albertus Medium	Body text	18	Bold, Number-ed	Left	24	6
Parahead	Paragraph headers	Albertus Medium	Body text	16	Bold	Left	12	6
Body text	Body text	Times New Roman	Body text	11	Normal	Left	0	6
Page Number	Header and Footer	Arial	Header	10	Normal	Left	0	0
Figure	Figure Caption	Times New Roman	Body text	10	Normal	Centre	6	6

Figure 11.20: A style sheet for a user manual

We will go through the procedure for creating the **Section** style. The procedure for creating all the other styles will be similar.

- From the **Format** menu select **Styles and Formatting**.

The Styles and Formatting Task pane is displayed.

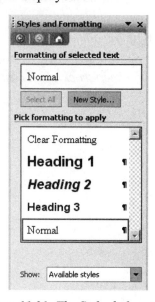

Figure 11.21: The Style dialogue box

- Click **New Style**. A dialogue box is displayed.

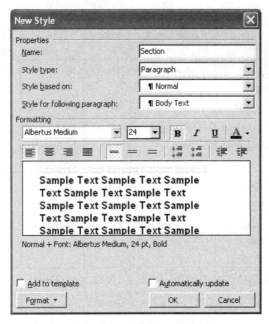

Figure 11.22: Creating a new style

- Fill it in as shown. The following style, **Body Text**, is a built-in style.

- Click the **Format** button and select **Paragraph**.

- Specify **Space Before** of **24** points, **Space After** of **6** points. Click **OK**.

- Click the **Format** button again and select **Numbering**. Click the **Numbered** tab, choose a suitable numbering style and change the indents if necessary by clicking the **Customise** button.

- Create the other styles in a similar manner by clicking **New Style** for each one.

- You can modify a style at any time by right-clicking on it in the Styles and Formatting Task pane and selecting **Modify**.

- Now select your **Section** style and type *Introduction*.

- Press **Enter** and the style should change automatically to **Body Text**. Type *The Holiday Cottage database is designed to let you keep track of all customers and holiday bookings etc...(further general overview.)*

11.11 Headers and footers

You will need to add a page number to each page.

- From the **View** menu select **Header and Footer**. A toolbar opens as shown in Figure 11.23.

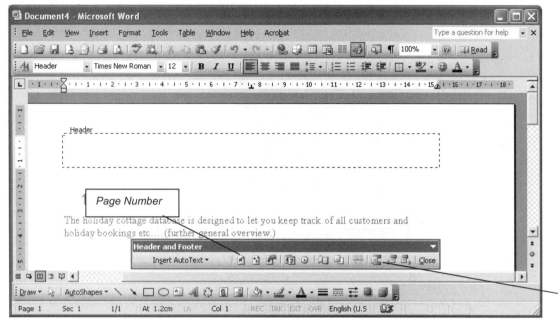

Figure 11.23: Inserting a header or footer

- If you want the page number at the bottom of the page rather than the top, click the **Switch between Header and Footer** button.

- Tab to go to the centre of the Footer.

- Select the **Page Number** icon on the Header and Footer toolbar. Click **Close** and the page number will be inserted at the bottom of each page in your user manual.

11.12 Screenshots

When you are describing how to use a piece of software, you will need to take screenshots and insert them into your document. There are many screen capture utility programs available which will let you capture just a single object or portion of the screen.

You can copy a picture of the whole screen to the clipboard by pressing the **Print Screen** key on the keyboard.

- Type the additional text as shown in Figure 11.24, using appropriate styles.

- Open your **NewCottages.mdb** database in Access, and the main menu should be displayed automatically.

- Press **PrintScreen** to copy a picture of the whole screen to the clipboard.

- Return to your user manual and paste it.

- You can crop the unwanted bits around it using the **Crop** tool on the Picture toolbar which appears when you select a picture.

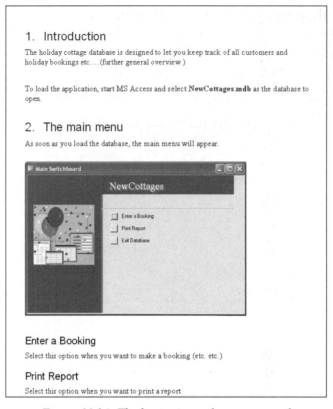

Figure 11.24: The beginnings of a user manual

11.13 Creating a table of contents

When you have finished writing your user manual, you should insert a table of contents at the beginning.

- Go to the beginning of the document.

- From the **Insert** menu select **Break**, **Page Break**.

- Go to the beginning of the document and type *Table of Contents*. Make it style **Heading 1**. Press **Enter** to go to a new line.

- From the **Insert** menu select **Reference**, **Index and Tables**. The following dialogue box is displayed.

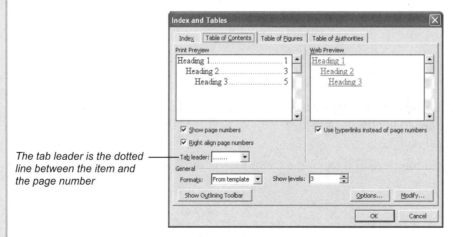

Figure 11.25: Inserting a table of contents

By default, any text in **Heading 1**, **Heading 2** and **Heading 3** style will be inserted into the table of contents. However, we want text in the styles **Section** and **Parahead** to appear in the TOC.

- Click **Options**. A further dialogue box is displayed.
- Delete the number **1** in the **Heading 1** box, **2** in **Heading 2** box and **3** in **Heading 3** box. These show the level of index entry. Make new entries as shown in Figure 11.26.

Figure 11.26: Specifying styles for TOC entries

- Click **OK**, and **OK** in the Index and Tables dialogue box. The TOC is inserted.
- You can select the whole TOC and alter the tabs so that it appears as shown in Figure 11.27.

Figure 11.27: The Table of Contents created automatically

When you add new text to the user manual, you will need to update the Table of Contents. You can do this by selecting it and pressing the function key **F9**.

That's the end of this task! The rest of the user manual is something you can work on yourself.

11.14 Relating this chapter to the specification

Specification Reference (Part B)	What you have done to satisfy this
IT3.1	
Plan how to obtain and use the information required for your tasks	• Planning the documents
Make selections based on judgements of relevance and quality.	• Get information from the user • Use the Internet to search for information • Choose appropriate information and confirm with the user
IT3.2	
Enter and bring together information using formats that help development	• Use of templates • Creating a style sheet • Headers and footers
Use software features to improve the efficiency of your work	• Mail merge • Conditional mail merge
Annotate/document your work to show that you have understood the processes followed and have taken account of the views of others	• Discussions with the user to get feedback on content, layout, format and style
IT3.3	
Develop the presentation so it is accurate, clear and presented consistently, taking account of the views of others	• Modify templates • Use of styles • Page numbers • Table of contents
Present your final output effectively using a format and style that suits your purpose and audience.	• Production of user manual • Production of stationery templates • Spell-checking and proof reading

11.15 Other Key Skills signposting

Communication   C3.3   Write a document about a complex subject, including an image.

11.16 Evidence for your portfolio

At level three you may choose to produce a word processing project. However, if this is to be your main substantial task then you may have to integrate it with other applications. Some examples have been suggested in this chapter, you could for example produce:

♦   a set of stationery templates for a local business

♦   a town centre guide describing locations and facilities together with photographs

- a mail merge using a standard letter produced in word and a data source from either Word or Access
- a user guide for a software package incorporating diagrams and screen shots
- a lengthy report, perhaps for your main area of study, incorporating tables, a table of contents and an index of entries
- a set of marketing sheets for a local business incorporating pictures, tables and charts showing the company's recent growth

Type of evidence	✔
Printouts of existing templates	
Rough sketches of page layouts	
Notes on information sources	
Notes of discussions with user	
Printouts of modified templates	
Printouts of mail merge documents (data source, master document and merged documents)	
Screenshots showing conditional merge in operation	
Screenshots showing the documents being saved	
A final printout (or screenshots) of menu, tables, forms, queries and reports	
Draft printouts of the user manual showing where corrections are required and why	
A copy of the completed user manual	
Record from your assessor of how you developed and presented the project	

11.17 Sample questions

You have been asked to produce a leaflet with two printed sides of A4 (landscape orientation) to publicise the opening of a new Sports Centre. The information should include the opening times, the facilities and the opening offers shown below. You should also include at least one suitable image on each side.

Facilities:	**Opening offers:**	**Opening times:**	
Swimming pool	Free sun bed session	Monday-Friday	8am-9pm
Jacuzzi	Half price swimming	Saturday	7am-10pm
Sauna and sun bed	Free squash racquet hire	Sunday	8am-9pm
Squash courts			

1.   On the first page include a large bold heading.
2.   Decide on the most appealing layout for the information given above.
3.   Incorporate at least one image on each page. Size these appropriately to fit with the text.
4.   Add a footer with your name, and with page numbers.
5.   Print out your work.
6.   Save your work and print a screenshot from Windows Explorer to show the saved file.

Chapter 12 – Desk Top Publishing and Web Page Design

Objectives

- ❑ Use Desk Top Publishing to produce a newsletter
- ❑ Incorporate text in columns, images, graphics and text wrap
- ❑ Convert the printed publication into web pages incorporating hyperlinks to other pages, and other sites
- ❑ Insert other design gallery objects such as a marquee, web buttons, etc.

Sample task: Create a newsletter for a Tennis Club and then convert it into web pages

In this chapter you will learn how to use the Desk Top Publishing (DTP) package Microsoft Publisher 2003, to create a printed newsletter for a local tennis club. Later you will convert the printed publication into web pages. You unlikely to be tested on these techniques but they will be useful for your portfolio evidence for Key Skill IT3.3 Present Information.

12.1 Planning the newsletter

Before you begin to get to grips with the software, you need to plan the publication. You clearly want it to look as professional as possible as it will be read, either in print or electronically, by quite a large number of people. Discuss the requirements with other people involved in the project before you start and ask them for feedback on drafts as you develop the project.

Things to consider may include the following:

♦ **Your intended audience and the purpose of the publication**
What age group is this aimed at? Is it just a Junior club for example? Is the publication required just for information, i.e. results listings and details of future fixtures, or is it intended to entertain as well? If so, you may include reports of matches and other social functions connected with the club.

♦ **Size of publication**
If you are intending to distribute a printed version of this newsletter, you may be restricted on length by the cost of production. You may also be limited by the amount of content you produce for the articles.

♦ **Layout of pages to ensure consistency of appearance**
The pages of the document (or web pages) should be designed to look as though they belong together by the use of a common layout (e.g. margins, font sizes and styles for body text and headings, use of formatting and colours, columns, indents etc.).

You should make notes of these considerations and draw out some rough sketches (by hand) of each page of the newsletter. Record your planning on a Planning record sheet and attach your notes and sketched plans.

12.2 Finding your information

It is likely that the items for a newsletter would come mainly from primary sources (see Chapter 6). For example, you may report first-hand from a tennis tournament or interview some club officials about a news item concerning a new clubhouse. Secondary sources might include some information about national championships that you have retrieved from the Internet or some photographs that a colleague has taken at a recent match and passed on to you.

Wherever you find the information, remember to record the sources (see the Information Seeking record sheet provided at www.payne-gallway.co.uk/ksit).

For the sample activity that follows in this chapter you are provided with some files that can be downloaded from the Payne-Gallway web site.

12.3 Using a wizard to create the basic newsletter

- To load Publisher, you can either click on the Publisher icon, or

- Click **Start**, **Programs**, then select **Microsoft Publisher**.

  The following screen will appear:

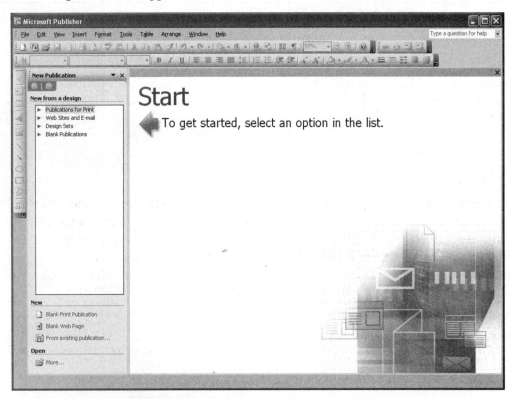

Figure 12.1: The opening screen in Publisher 2003

- Click on **Publications for Print** in the list on the left and then select **Newsletters**. A series of newsletter layouts will appear. You can browse through these to select a suitable one. However, for this activity click on the one labelled **Borders** newsletter.

- If this is the first time you have used Publisher, a message box will appear requiring you to enter your Personal Information. Either enter your details, or press **Cancel**.

The following screen will appear:

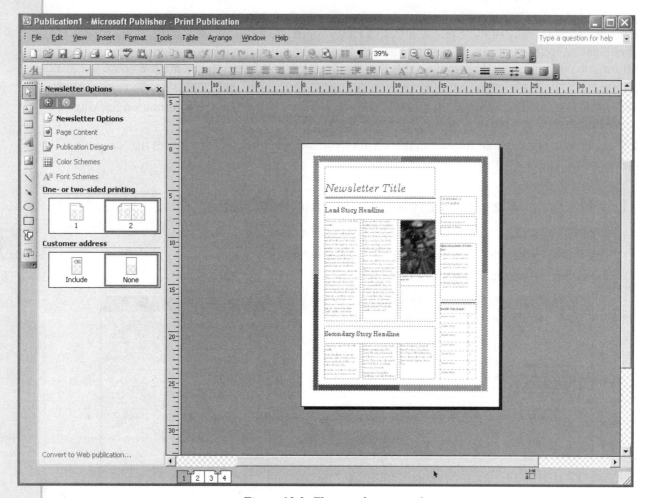

Figure 12.2: The newsletter template

The basic newsletter template is displayed on the screen.

- Choose to print your document on single sides. A message will appear telling you that Publisher is modifying the pages of your publication to match the specified layout. Click **Yes**.
- Click on **Color Schemes** and select a new colour scheme if you wish.
- Click on **Page Content** and select **3** columns.
- Select **File**, **Save As** and save the document as **Tennis**.

Now the basic publication is ready to edit. Your screen should look something like this:

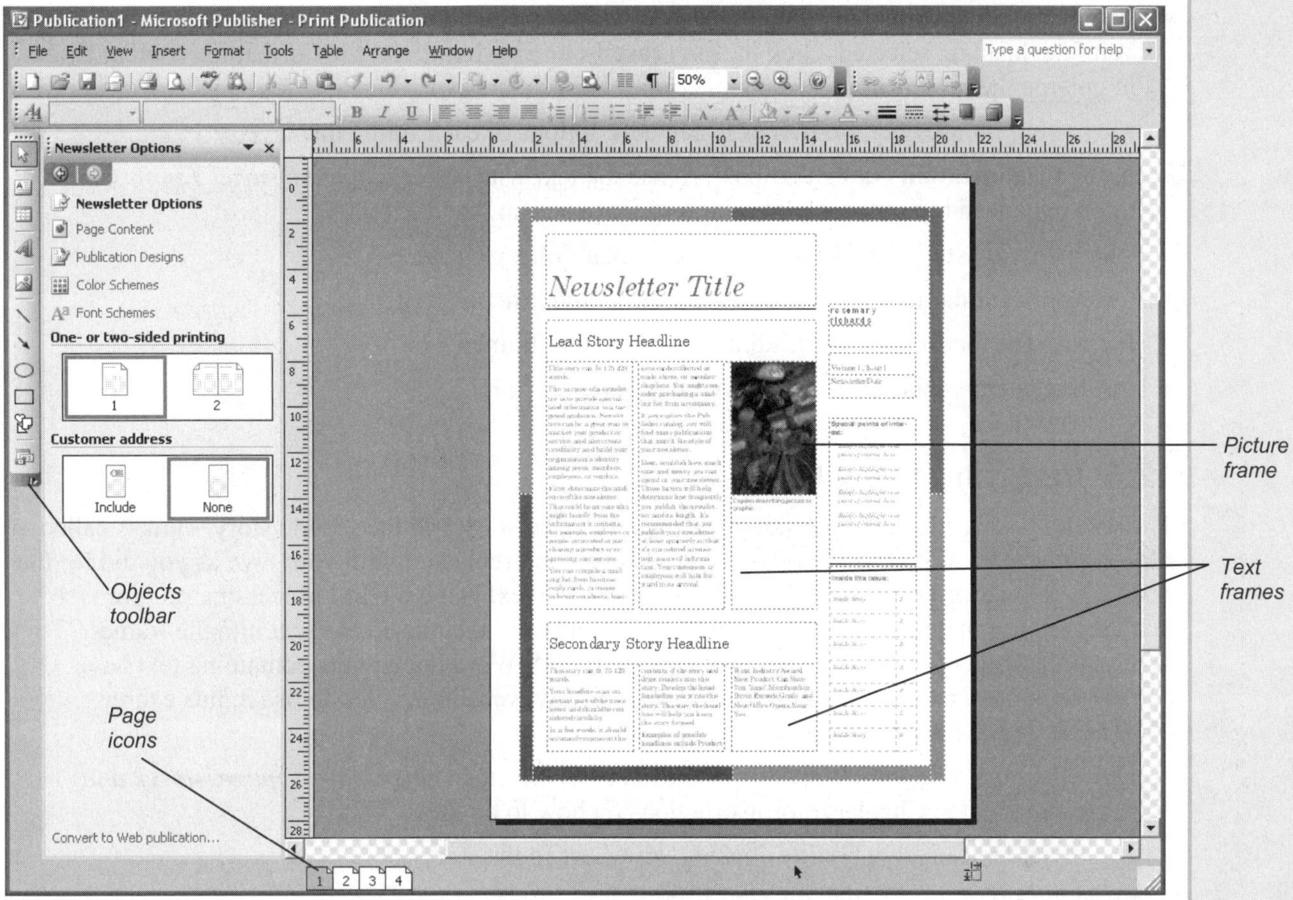

Figure 12.3: The basic publication ready to edit

You will see that the publication is split into frames. The basic method of working with Publisher is by using two types of frame, a text frame (or text box) and an object (or Picture) frame. You have to create a frame to contain anything you want to add to your page. You can use the **Text Box** tool, the **Insert Table** tool or the **Picture Frame** tool from the Objects toolbar to create frames as required. These can then be moved, sized or deleted like other objects. However, in this activity the document template has created all of the frames for you. The template has created 4 pages – try clicking on the page numbers at the bottom of the screen to see how it has formatted the other pages.

12.4 Deleting pages of the publication

We only want 2 pages in the newsletter, so we will delete pages 3 and 4.

- Click on the icon for page number 4. From the **Edit** menu select **Delete Page**.

- Click on the icon for page number 3. From the **Edit** menu select **Delete Page**. The icons for pages 1 and 2 should still be displayed.

12.5 Editing the heading text

- Ensure page 1 is displayed. Highlight the text **Newsletter Title** and replace with *Tennis Times*. With the heading selected, click the **Increase Font Size** button on the Formatting toolbar twice to enlarge the masthead.

- Move your mouse over the frames to see descriptions of each frame displayed.

- In the **Organization Name** text box replace the text with *Bergfield and District Tennis Club.* (You may need to use the **Zoom** button so that you can read the text.)

- Change **Lead Story Headline** to *Club awarded Lottery Grant.*

- Change **Secondary Story Headline** to *New Clubhouse on the way.*

- Increase the font size of the headlines to fit the text frames.

- Insert a date to replace the text **Newsletter Date**.

12.6 Inserting body text

The wizard has inserted some standard text into the lead story and the second story – this is called **placeholder text**. It is possible to highlight this text and replace it with your own as you did for the headings. However it is often a good idea to create the text using a word processing program (so that you can use the various tools within that program) and then insert the text into the frames. To save you the bother of typing in reams of text, some MS Word documents containing text have already been prepared and saved on the Payne-Gallway web site for you to use in this exercise. *("And here is one I prepared earlier!")*

- Download the following Word files: *leadstory, secondstory, page2story1, page2story2 and page2story3.* See Chapter 6 for instructions on how to do this.

- Highlight the lead story text by clicking anywhere in the story.

- From the **Insert** menu click on **Text File**.

- Browse through the folders on your hard disk drive to find the file *leadstory.*

- Click on the filename **leadstory** and then click **OK**.

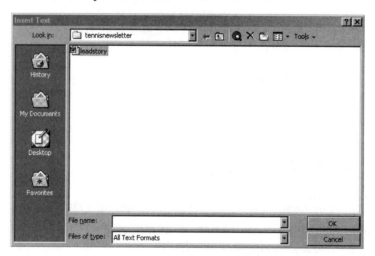

Figure 12.4: Insert text file dialogue box

The story about the new lottery grant should be inserted into the first three columns.

If you get a message informing you that 'Publisher can't import the specified format' it means that when the software was installed, the necessary filters were not installed. They can be installed from the original CD-ROM. Alternatively, use the .txt versions of the files on the website.

You may also find that you get the following message:

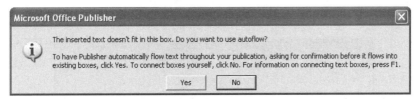

Figure 12.5: Overflow text message

- Click **No**, as you don't want this story flowing into any further text boxes.
- Either make the text smaller or click on the **Line Spacing** button and change the spacing between lines and paragraphs until the text fits in.

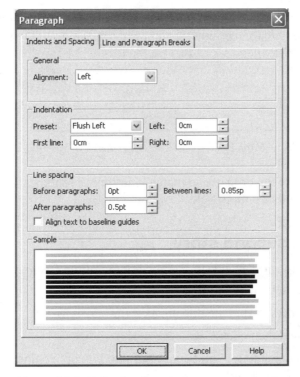

Figure 12.6: Adjusting line and paragraph spacing

12.7 Inserting an image

The template has inserted a picture of a cyclist within the lead story. This needs to be replaced with a more appropriate picture.

- Click the picture frame to select it and then press the **Delete** key.
- From the **Insert** menu, click **Picture** and then **Clip Art.**
- Search for an appropriate picture and click on it to insert it**.**

Note that you can drag the picture to move it, or size it with the black selection handles.

12.8 Inserting a drop cap

A drop cap is a large dropped initial capital letter inserted at the beginning of a paragraph.

- Make sure the insertion point is before the first character in the first paragraph and select **Format**, **Drop Cap**.

- Select the second option on the left of the **drop cap** dialogue box and click **OK**.

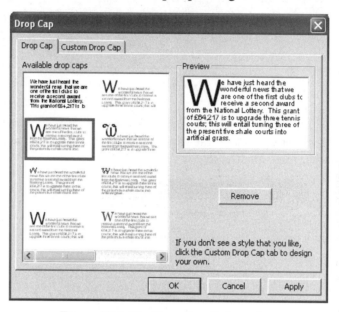

Figure 12.7: The Drop Cap dialogue box

- Now change the colour of the drop cap to match your colour scheme. Select the drop cap and click the **Font Color** toolbar button. Select a colour.

12.9 Inserting the second story

- Highlight the columns for the second story at the bottom of the first page.

- From the **Insert** menu click on **Text File**.

- Browse through the folders to find the downloaded file *secondstory*.

- Click on the filename and then click **OK**.

- The story about the new clubhouse will be inserted into the three columns. However, this text is also too long to fit into the available space. Publisher asks you if you would like to **autoflow** onto another page. Click **No** and adjust the text size and spacing as you did for the lead story.

12.10   Completing the front page

- Replace the placeholder text in the text box entitled **Special points of interest:** with a bulleted list of fictional diary dates for the clubhouse opening, junior tournament etc. We will fill in the Contents panel when the rest of the newsletter is complete.

- From the **View** menu, de-select **Boundaries and Guides.** The text box lines should disappear. Your newsletter front page should now look something like this:

Figure 12.8: The front page

12.11   The second page

- Click on the **Page 2** icon at the bottom of the screen to view the second page of the newsletter.

The template has inserted placeholder text for three stories and two pictures on this page. Use the techniques described in the sections above to replace the placeholder text with **page2story1**, **page2story2** and **page2story3** in the appropriate text boxes.

> **Note:**   For **page2story1**, delete the two text boxes and use the **Text box** tool on the Objects toolbar to create one text box to fill the space. Change the size of the font to **12**pt.

Leave the first picture, but download the second picture (**page2image2**) from the web site. Refer to chapter 6 for instructions on how to download this file to your computer and then insert it onto page 2 of the newsletter as follows:

- Click on the placeholder image at the bottom of the page in the third story.
- Note that the caption is set up as a text box that has been grouped together with the picture frame. These frames need to be ungrouped as follows:
- With the picture frame selected click the **Ungroup Objects** icon beneath the caption.

- Select just the picture and delete it.
- From the **Insert** menu, select **Picture, From File**.
- Browse through the folders until you find the downloaded file you want to insert. Click on the filename and then click **Insert**. Size the picture to fit

We want the pictures on page 2 to have captions. Enter the following captions:

- For the first image, type *The Girls champion, Joy Todd* in the caption text box.
- For **page2image2**, type *The LTA web site* in the caption text box.

In the middle of **page2story2** there is another text box for a **pull quote** - this is a piece of text that you insert as a quote in a larger font size, and is designed to catch the reader's attention. Insert it as follows:

- Highlight the placeholder pull quote text. Overwrite this with the following text (italic, 14pt Times New Roman): *"Their involvement will be sorely missed"*
- Enter the story headlines as shown in figure 12.9.

Your second page should now look something like this:

Figure 12.9: The completed page 2

12.12   The contents list

- Return to the front page of the newsletter by clicking on the **Page 1** icon at the bottom of the screen.

- Overwrite the placeholder text in the contents list so that it looks like this:

Inside this issue:

Lottery Grant	*1*
New Clubhouse	*1*
Diary dates	*1*
Junior Tournament Results	*2*
Retirement	*2*
Wimbledon Championships	*2*
Inside Story	*6*

Figure 12.10: The newsletter contents

This text box has been set up as a table. We do not require the last cell in the table.

- Drag over the last row of the table to select it.

- From the **Table** menu, select **Delete Rows.**

The newsletter is now complete and the two pages should look like this:

Figure 12.11: The completed newsletter

12.13   Printing the newsletter

- From the **File** menu select **Print**.
- Select to print both pages in the **Print Dialogue** box.
- **Save** and **close** your newsletter file.

12.14   Creating web pages from the newsletter publication

Because you have created a newsletter using one of the Publisher 2003 templates, you can convert the publication into web pages very quickly and easily.

- Open the newsletter publication (**Tennis.pub**).
- Select **File**, **Convert to Web Publication**.

You are asked if you want to save the publication before converting it.

- Click **Yes** and then click **Next**.
- In the next dialogue box select the option **No, do not add a navigation bar** and then click **Finish**.

The print publication will now be converted to a web publication. You will immediately spot a problem – text wrapping is not available in web publications, so your graphic on page 1 and the pull-out quote on page 2 will be covering some text. You will have to modify your design slightly to accommodate this problem. Size and move the text boxes and objects until you are happy with the layout.

You are now going to insert some hyperlinks from the contents list to the second page. You will then insert some hyperlinks on the second page to return to the first page.

- In the Contents list, highlight the entry for the Junior tournament results.
- From the **Insert** menu, select **Hyperlink**.
- In the Hyperlink dialogue box click on **Link to: Place in this Document**. Click on **Page 2**. Click **OK**.
- Repeat this process to add hyperlinks to the last two entries in the contents list.
  The three items in the contents list should now have changed to blue underlined text – the default style for hyperlinks.

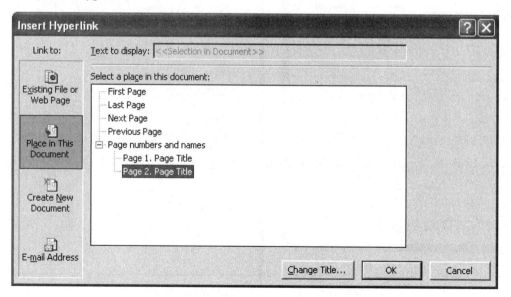

Figure 12.12: The hyperlink dialogue box

- Now click on the Page 2 icon.
- At the end of each of the three stories on page 2 draw a separate text box using the **Text Box Tool**.
- Enter the text **Return to first page** in each of the new text frames.
- Highlight the first of these entries.
- From the **Insert** menu, select **Hyperlink**.
- In the **Hyperlink** dialogue box, click on **Link to: Place in this Document**.
- Click on **First Page**. Click **OK**.
- Repeat this process to add hyperlinks to the text in the other two new text boxes.

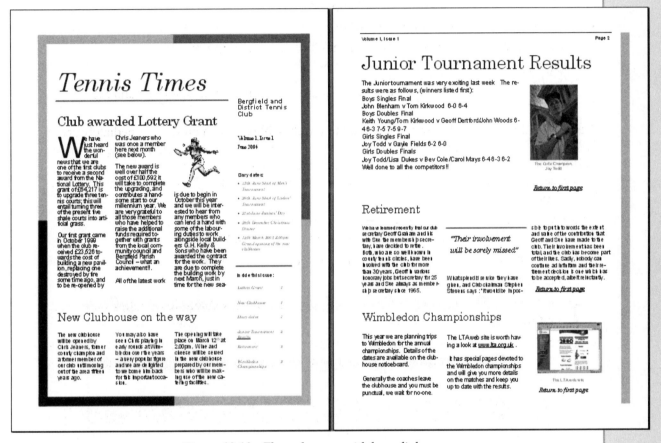

Figure 12.13: The web pages with hyperlinks

Now you can create a hyperlink to the LTA (Lawn Tennis Association) web site.

- Select the LTA web site address in the last story on the second page.
- From the **Insert** menu select **Hyperlink**.
- Click on **Link to: Existing File or Web Page**. Type *www.lta.org.uk* as the Internet address of the web site or file, and click **OK**.

12.15   Saving the web site

- From the **File** menu, select **Save As**. Select File as type **Web Page**. Save as *webpagenewsletter*.
- Click Save. This will have saved the document as an html file.

12.16   Testing your web site

- Open **webpagenewsletter** in Publisher, and then select **File**, **Web Page Preview**.
- Publisher generates your pages as a web site, and then opens it in your default web browser (e.g. Internet Explorer). Test the site to ensure that:
    - ♦ Text is visible and legible.
    - ♦ Images are visible on each page and download quickly.
    - ♦ The hyperlinks work and take the user to the expected destinations.

12.17   Adding Design Gallery Objects

The Design Gallery contains an assortment of Publisher-designed objects, such as borders, pull quotes, logos, web buttons and marquees that you can add to your publication.

You will find that when the pages are displayed in the browser the edges of the second page are not well defined. It would look better if the pages had a border.

- From the menu select **File, Close** to close the Web page preview. The publication will remain open.
- Click the **Page 1** icon to display the first page.
- From the **Insert** menu select **Design Gallery Objects**.
- Click on **Borders** in the **Categories** list.
- Insert the border selected in the figure below, by selecting it and then clicking **Insert Object**.
- Reposition and size the border around the page.
- Repeat for page 2.
- **Save** the file.

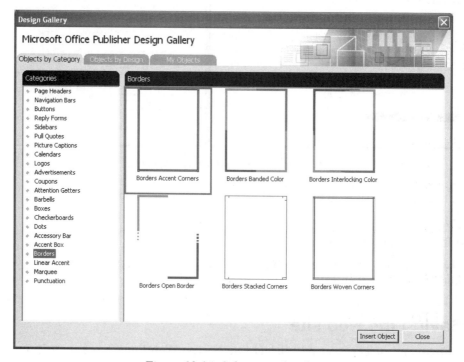

Figure 12.14: Selecting a border

Now we will replace the hyperlinks on page 2 of the newsletter with web buttons and add a decorative marquee.

- On page 2 of the newsletter delete the text frames containing the hyperlinks to return you to page 1. (To do this, click on the text frame to select it, right-click to display the shortcut menu and select **Delete Object**.)

Insert web buttons as follows:

- From the **Insert** menu select **Design Gallery Object**.
- Click on **Buttons** in the **Categories** list.
- Insert the **Home** button selected in the figure below by clicking on it and then clicking **Insert Object**.

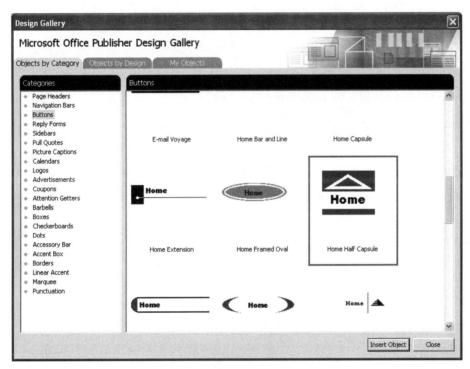

Figure 12.15: Selecting a web button

- Position the button at the end of the first story.
- Replace the caption **Home** with **First Page**.
- Place similar buttons at the end of the other two stories on page 2.
- Save the file.
- Click **Web Page Preview** from the **File** menu.
- Test out your web buttons.

Add a decorative marquee

- On page 1 of the newsletter, move the text boxes so that you have some white space underneath the masthead **Tennis Times**.
- From the **Insert** menu select **Design Gallery Object**.
- Click on **Marquee** in the **Categories** list.
- Insert the marquee selected in the figure below by selecting it and then clicking **Insert Object**.

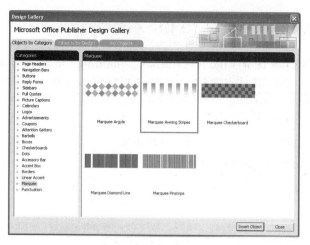

Figure 12.16: Selecting a marquee

- Move and size the marquee so that it stretches across the page.

Your completed pages should look something like this:

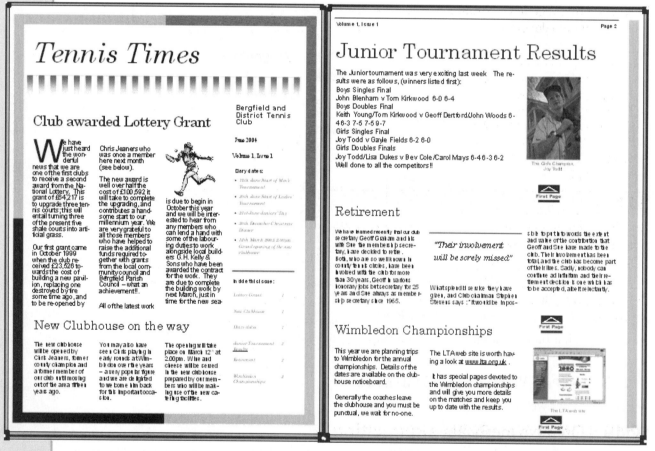

Figure 12.17: The completed pages

- Remember to save your work.

12.18   Relating this chapter to the specification

Specification Reference (Part B)	What you have done to satisfy this
IT3.1	
Plan how to obtain and use the information required for your tasks	• Planning the newsletter production
Make selections based on judgements of relevance and quality.	• Download text files from web site • Find Clip Art files • Interviewing people • Observation • Take photographs • Selecting appropriate images and text
IT3.2	
Enter and bring together information using formats that help development	• Use of templates • Insertion and sizing of images • Formatting the publication
Use software features to improve the efficiency of your work	• Conversion of publication into a web page • Use of hyperlinks
Annotate/document your work to show that you have understood the processes followed and have taken account of the views of others	• Access by others to the web pages • Discussing the project with others
IT3.3	
Develop the presentation so it is accurate, clear and presented consistently, taking account of the views of others	• Editing text • Adding design gallery objects
Present your final output effectively using a format and style that suits your purpose and audience.	• Refining the layout and formatting of the publication and the web site • Spell-checking the publication • Testing the web site • Getting user feedback

12.19   Other Key Skills signposting

Communication   C3.1   Read and synthesise information from a document (including an image).

C3.3   Write a document about a complex subject, including an image.

12.20   Evidence for your portfolio

Desktop publishing applications will provide many opportunities for producing evidence for your portfolio. You could for example choose to produce:

♦   a newsletter similar to the one created in this chapter for your own school, club, class etc.

♦   a calendar of events

♦   a programme of events for a Sports day, a theatrical production, etc.

♦   a sales catalogue for a local business

♦   advertisements, posters, flyers, tickets for a school/college event

♦   a web page for your school, college or club.

Type of evidence	✔
A written description of the activity	
Rough sketches of the publication layout	
Rough sketches of the web pages' layout and navigation links	
Notes on sources of information for newsletter items (including notes of any interviews you conduct)	
Notes on sources of images	
Working drafts of the publication showing corrections required and why	
Working drafts of web pages showing corrections required and why	
A final printout of the publication	
A final printout of the web pages	
Record from your assessor of how you developed and presented the project	

12.21   Sample questions

In this exercise you are asked to produce an invitation to a fund-raising event at your school or college. The publication will be based on a Microsoft Publisher template. You are then asked to convert the document into web pages with appropriate links to allow you to navigate between the pages.

Task 1

1.   Create an invitation using one of the Fundraiser invitation templates, updating the Personal Information with your school or college details.
2.   Replace the placeholder text with some appropriate text.
3.   Insert some pictures from the Clip Art Gallery.
4.   Print the pages.

Task 2

1.   Convert the pages of your invitation into web pages.
2.   Adjust any formatting as necessary.
3.   Add hyperlinks so that you can move between pages.
4.   Test your web pages in Internet Explorer and demonstrate them to your teacher.

Appendix

QCA
Specifications
for Levels
2 and 3

Level 2, Part A
YOU NEED TO KNOW HOW TO:

- identify errors *(eg in hardware and software you are using)* and their causes
- observe copyright and/or confidentiality when it is necessary
- how to minimise health risks
- how to minimise risks from viruses
- send and receive email

Find and select information

- identify suitable sources of information *(e.g. written documents, material to be scanned, files, CD ROMs, the Internet)*
- search for information using multiple search criteria *(e.g. using AND or '<' and '>', or tools such as search engines)*
- interpret information and select what you need for different purposes *(e.g. to respond to an enquiry, write a project report, design or make something).*

Develop information

- enter and combine information *(e.g. copy and paste or insert text, images and number)*, using formats that help development *(e.g. using table structures, text boxes or text wrap to position information)*
- develop information in the form of text, images and numbers *(eg organise information under headings, structure tables, generate charts and graphs from data, use queries to select records)*
- derive new information *(e.g. compare information from different sources to reach a conclusion, use formulas to calculate information such as a total or average).*

Present information

- select and use layouts and techniques to suit different tasks *(e.g. document structures such as indents, columns and headings, borders for images and text, tables, highlight information to improve its impact, make sure it suits the needs of the audience)*
- develop the presentation to suit your purpose and audience and the types of information used ie. text, images and numbers *(e.g. format information to improve its impact, refine layout making sure it suits the needs of your audience)*
- present information in a consistent way *(e.g. paragraph layouts, sizes and styles of text, alignment, fonts).*
- ensure your work is accurate and clear.

Level 2, Part B
YOU MUST:

- ❑ Carry out two activities which include tasks for all three of IT2.1, IT2.2 and IT2.3

Overall, through two or more activities you must:
- ❑ include at least one IT-based information source
- ❑ include at least one non-IT based information source
- ❑ use at least one example of text, one example of image and one example of number
- ❑ present evidence of purposeful use of email

You must:	Evidence must show you can:
IT2.1 Search for and select information to meet your needs. Use different information sources for each activity and multiple search criteria in at least one case.	• **select information relevant to the tasks.**
IT2.2 Enter and develop the information and derive new information.	• **enter and combine information using formats that help development;** • **develop information and derive new information as appropriate.**
IT2.3 Present combined information such as text with image, text with number, image with number.	• **develop the presentation so that the final output is accurate and shows consistent use of formats;** • **use layout appropriate to the types of information.**

Level 3, Part A
YOU NEED TO KNOW HOW TO:

- ❑ save your work for easy retrieval and to avoid loss, using version management
- ❑ how to minimise health risks
- ❑ how to minimise risks from viruses
- ❑ send and receive email with attachments

Find and select information

- ❑ plan and organise your work *(e.g. by use of subdirectories/subfolders)*
- ❑ select sources of information which are suitable for your purpose *(e.g. spreadsheets containing sales figures, a database containing customer details, a web page of product details)*
- ❑ choose appropriate search techniques for finding information efficiently *(e.g. database query techniques and multiple search criteria).*

Develop information

- ❑ enter information in consistent formats *(e.g. using font styles, data formats, table structures)*
- ❑ use software features to improve the efficiency of your work *(e.g. mail merge, database queries, validation of database entries and LOOKUP functions within spreadsheets)*
- ❑ create and use structures and procedures for developing and combining text, images and numbers *(eg group and sort information, use spreadsheet software to generate graphs and charts)*
- ❑ derive new information *(e.g. a document incorporating information from a variety of sources, a spreadsheet to calculate results using conditional statements with logical operators and other formulas).*

Present information

- ❑ develop the structure of your presentation *(e.g. modify templates and paragraph styles, apply automatic referencing facilities such as page numbers, dates and filenames)*
- ❑ develop and refine your presentation by combining text, images and numbers *(e.g. improve impact by changing format for layouts, use of slide transition features, use of hyperlinks in web pages)*
- ❑ present information so that it meets your purpose and the needs of the audience *(e.g. from spreadsheets, selected mail merge printouts, database reports of grouped information).*

Level 3, Part B
YOU MUST:

❑ Show that you can **plan** and carry through a number of different tasks, one of which must be a major task covering IT3.1, IT3.2 and IT3.3.

Each component, IT3.1, IT3.2 and IT3.3, must be covered at least twice, and IT3.3 must be covered for at least two different audiences. Smaller tasks may be used to ensure each component is covered.

Overall through at least two activities you must:
❑ include at least one IT based information source
❑ include at least one non IT based information source
❑ use at least one example of text, one example of image and one example of number
❑ use one example of combined information such as text and number, or image and number or text and image
❑ present evidence of sending and receiving email; one of these emails must have an attachment related to the task.

You must:	Evidence must show you can:
IT3.1 Search for information, using different sources, and multiple search criteria in at least one case.	• **plan how to obtain and use the information required for your tasks;** • **make selections based on judgements of relevance and quality.**
IT3.2 Enter and develop the information and derive new information. .	• **enter and bring together information using formats that help development;** • **use software features to improve the efficiency of your work;** • **annotate/document your work to show that you have understood the processes followed and have taken account of the views of others.**
IT3.3 Present the information.	• **develop the presentation so it is accurate, clear and presented consistently, taking account of the views of others;** • **present your final output effectively using a format and style that suits your purpose and audience.**

Index